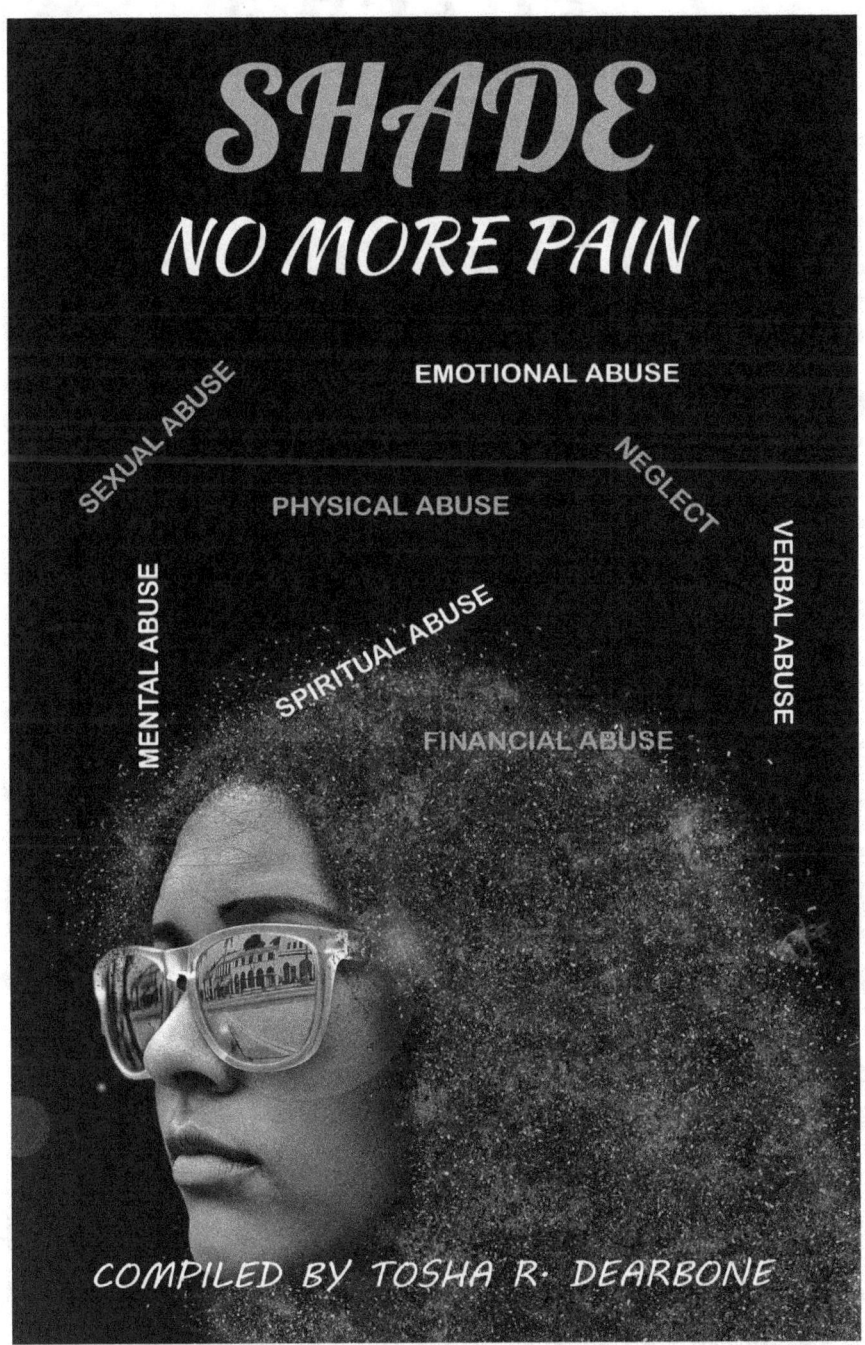

Tosha R. Dearbone

SHADE: NO MORE PAIN

Compiled By:
Tosha R. Dearbone

Contributions From (in order of appearance):

Nikki Jackson
Dewana Munoz
Katrina Garrett
Tearini Hubert
Reyna Harris-Goynes
Delanishia Woods
LaTonya L. Jones
Joslyn Curley
Tragula Speaks

Redemption's Story Publishing, LLC, Houston, Texas

Shade: No More Pain

Shade: No More Pain

Copyright © 2019
Tosha R. Dearbone

All Rights Reserved.
No portion of this publication may be reproduced, stored in any electronic system, or transmitted in any form or by any means (electronic, mechanical, photocopy, recording, or otherwise) without written permission from the publisher. Brief quotations may be used in literary reviews.

Print ISBN 13: 978-1-947445-53-6
Library of Congress Control Number: 2019902816

Scripture references are taken from the English Standard Version (ESV) and New International Version (NIV) of the Holy Bible and used with permission by Zondervan via Biblegateway.com.
Public Domain.

For information and bulk ordering, contact,
Redemption's Story Publishing, LLC
Angela Edwards, CEO
P.O. Box 62287
Houston, TX 77205
RedeemedByHim@Redemptions-Story.com

DEDICATION

To every young girl and young lady of Positive Express:

This book of experiences is dedicated to you.
May you learn, release, heal, and grow from it.

Know that you are worthy and valuable
each and every day of your life.

Tosha R. Dearbone

Web: www.trdearbo.wix.com/positiveexpress

Email: positive.express.14@gmail.com

Facebook: www.facebook.com/positiveexpress

ACKNOWLEDGMENTS

I want to first give honor and thanks to **God** for this opportunity to sow into the lives of all who read this amazing piece of literary art.

To each of the women who shared their experiences in *Shade: No More Pain*: You are beyond words of greatness!

A special thank you to my "Spiritual Mother," **Pastor Clara L. Peters,** for such a beautiful Foreword. To read it and see the impartation you have displayed upon my life is nothing short of remarkable. I am honored to have you in my life. I can say with all honesty that you are the one who began my transformation process. God bless you.

To **Angela Edwards**, CEO of Redemption's Story Publishing, LLC: Thank you for all of your hard work in assembling this project and for working alongside each one of us as we shared our stories. With your dedication and passion behind this collaborative work, we are grateful for your services.

Last but not least, I want to thank **my children** for being by my side through it all. You saw things in me that I didn't even see in myself. I love all of you and my grandbaby.

Tosha R. Dearbone

FOREWORD

"May the God of hope fill you with all joy and peace in believing, so that by the power of the Holy Spirit you may abound in hope."
~ **Romans 15:13, ESV** ~

As I sit pondering on what I will pen for the Foreword for this book, I think back to when Tosha Dearbone contacted me with her request to write the Foreword. I was honored to be asked and thankful to be chosen by God to share the story that put me in a position to write this.

Tosha has been one of my spiritual daughters for many years. I am proud that she found her voice to speak up and out regarding abuse, self-esteem issues, and HIV. I pray as this book is compiled with the many testimonies, that the messages shared with the world are heard according to how God has designed for the vision of this book.

Many people refuse to share their story because they feel they will be ridiculed and that their past "situations" will stop them from heading to where God has already shifted them. I believe that the women who decided to come forth and share their testimony are sharing because they are on assignment from the **LORD** to help save girls, young women, and women from the life of tragedy that they have experienced.

In sharing my testimony, I have learned that some people still believe "it will **NEVER** happen to them" because they believe they are "above or better than the next woman." No one sets out to be abused. They are not the abuser; they are the victim. Abuse happens **TO** them. One never knows what the future holds. However, we find ourselves trusting the one who says they love us and made a vow to love—yet abuse is on their own selfish agenda *(I say 'agenda' to be nice, but you get what I'm saying)*. People who abuse do it because of their own undealt with "issues" from their youth or the idea that they can say or do anything to the victim—and the victim should just go along with it.

Well, I come to tell you that it is **NOT** okay. Our Heavenly Father did **NOT** create us to be used and abused by ***ANYONE***!

I share my personal testimony of abuse not because I want to expose my abuser, but because I want to help others who are being abused to know and understand that God has something better for them. Please do not just "settle" because you don't want to be alone. Being alone is better than being with someone who abuses you whenever it feels right to them. It is unhealthy to be in a relationship where you are always uptight and unsure about how your abuser will be when you are in their presence.

"He heals the brokenhearted and binds up their wounds."
~ Psalms 147:3, NIV ~

I want to encourage each woman who reads this book to imagine being 'that woman' who has gone through their unique abuse situations and see what you can do to improve your own life. Make sure you are not missing the mark of knowing your worth and what **GOD** has said about them. Pay attention to the stories shared within, as you may find that someone within your circle could be suffering the same abuse in silence. Share this book with her. Help her understand her value and let her know she needs to execute a plan to take her life back.

Many women give in to being mistreated because when they are not, it feels as if they are unloved. When not being abused, they may think, *"No one has ever shown me* **this** *type of love."* Thoughts then lean toward, **"THIS** *is the love I've been searching for!"* All the while, they feel invisible. As women, we sometimes just go along with "whatever" because we don't want to struggle alone. By doing this, we are giving up on self and just existing in this life. Existing in life is not what was ordained for us. We were not put here to be in bondage.

You may feel as though you have nothing to live for, but trust this: God will restore you to **YOU**. Trust the process as He releases you from bondage.

"Trust in the Lord with all your heart, and do not lean on your own understanding. In all your ways, acknowledge Him, and He will make straight your paths."
~ Proverbs 3:5-6, ESV ~

As in the Book of Ruth, Naomi's restoration came through Ruth by her gleaning in Boaz's field. Ruth found favor while gleaning. Ruth 3:1 reads, *"My daughter, shall I not seek security for you that it may be well with you?"* Naomi saw hope at that time and gave Ruth some instructions to follow. It was then that restoration began for Naomi. To her, she had no life left to live. Furthermore, Ruth 4:15 states, *"And may he be to you a restorer of life and a nourisher of your old age; for your daughter-in-law, who loves you, who is better to you than seven sons, has borne him."* Naomi was truly on her way back to being called

"Naomi" again (not Mara), as God was restoring her life after one filled with tragedy.

Just as God restored Naomi, He will do the same for you. He will give you your life back full of peace, joy, happiness, and love. Life after abuse is beautiful, and I love sharing with women *AND* men that life is not over just because they went through hell to find peace.

Shade: No More Pain was written to show women that their lives matter. Their dreams and all that God has for them matters. They should not sacrifice who they are for another just to make them feel desired.

Yes, we (as women) are to submit to our spouse — **BUT** we are not to be controlled. So, I encourage you today: If your mate (husband or boyfriend) is controlling you mentally, verbally, emotionally, physically, financially, or even spiritually, you must stop the behavior and ask him to get help. Tell him you will not be a part of that lifestyle any longer, as that is **NOT** what you signed up for. Make sure he understands that you refuse to go another day, another month, or even another year being with a man who says he loves you while abusing you, all because he feels he can. Help him to understand that you deserve better and would prefer to live the rest of your life alone than to live a life of bondage and abuse.

I also encourage you to have open communication daily so that each of you can be on the same page. As women, we know what we want and need. We know what we are willing to do for our mate in the relationship; however, abuse is never acceptable. Women, speak up! If we don't, we will always allow someone to abuse us. Abuse can only continue if we allow it, so let's **STOP** it…*NOW!*

Right now, I ask that **YOU**:

1. Forgive yourself for allowing "that person" to abuse you.
2. Promise to fall in love with **YOU**.
3. Live life to the fullest according to God.
4. Give yourself permission to say *"YES!"* to you.
5. Stand in the mirror and say, "*(Insert your name here)*, it's time to take control over your life!"

GOD wants you to know that you have to sometimes go through the wilderness to see the greatness He has for you. Don't let your naysayers stop you from being restored into what **GOD**—*not MAN*—has promised you. Live life to the fullest by living, laughing, and loving with no **REGRETS**, as tomorrow is not promised. You owe it to yourself to live the life God created for you.

Decree and declare today and always: **"I WILL WIN!"**

"For I know the plans I have for you, declares the Lord, plans for welfare and not for evil, to give you a future and a hope."
~ **Jeremiah 29:11, ESV** ~

Blessings and Love,

Pastor Clara L. Peters.

TABLE OF CONTENTS

Dedication vi
Acknowledgements vii
Foreword by Pastor Clara L. Peters viii

Nikki Jackson 1
   Dear God, Why Me? 2

Dewana Munoz 11
   The Secrets I Held Within 12

Katrina Garrett 25
   Unconsciously Silenced 26

Tosha R. Dearbone 37
   Too Silent to be Heard 38

Tearini Hubert 49
   But You Love Me, Though… 50

Reyna Harris-Goynes 63
   In the Midst of it All 64

Delanishia Woods 75
   History Repeated: Broken By Hope 76

LaTonya L. Jones 89
   No Pain, No Gain 90

Joslyn Curley 101
   Unchained 102

Tragula Speaks 113
   New Life is Just Over the Horizon 114
   Conclusion 127
   Appendix 130

Tosha R. Dearbone

Shade: No More Pain

Nikki Jackson

*"So many people don't know that God loves them.
They feel, 'Why would God love me?
Why would He be interested in me?"
~ Jan Karon ~*

DEAR GOD, WHY ME?

It's often said that time heals all wounds, but what about the pain that lies ahead? Is this the plan you have for my life, God? What did I do to deserve this? Is this how this Christian walk is supposed to be? Explain it to me, God. I served your people, prayed day in and day out, attended church all day Tuesday and both services on Sunday. What did I miss in the process? God, I need to hear from You! *God, Why ME? Why ME, God?*

I have asked myself those questions over and over.

As I sit in this room staring at the four walls, I am trying to wrap my mind around how I got here. I had it all. I am a Business Professional with the perfect husband, three amazing kids, a home, a driveway full of cars, my own businesses, and travel around the world at any given time—yet here I am broke, broken, bruised, empty, lifeless, and lonely. How did my life change in the blink of an eye? What devil in Hell came and destroyed my entire life? This must be a horrible dream that has trapped me into believing my fairytale marriage is in trouble. Not me! How can I ever face the people who look up to me? If they knew all of what I'm going through, I would be the talk of the town and most definitely on social media.

Then, it hits me. This is all too familiar. The difference is that this time, it didn't come with a warning sign. What I mean is that every other time I did something Mr. Perfect didn't like, I paid for it either physically, mentally, or emotionally. We all recognize those three components of **Domestic Violence**.

There was the time I came home late after attending his cousin's party. When I opened the door, he was standing on the other side. The look on his face, the rage in his eyes, and the trembling of his bottom lip let me know: I was in for it. I can't fail to mention this was the very first time he abused me.

When I woke up in the hospital hours later, nurses and the police surrounded my bed. When they asked what happened and I told them, I was encouraged to lie—not just to keep him out of jail, but also to save my life. Who thinks that way? Surely not me! If I didn't know anything else, I knew that man loved my dirty underwear. But does love really hurt? I mean hurt to the point where you are walking on eggshells because you don't want to piss off Mr. Perfect.

As a child, I was taught that what goes on in the house stays in the house. Honestly, I had no one I could really tell because, over time, I lost the majority of my friends. Hell, I even lost **ME**! I was the one who held it down for everyone else and ensured they were okay before my needs were met. That's what I was supposed to do, right? **WRONG!** While loving him, it started to kill me (not physically; I was dying slowly on the inside deep in my *soul*).

I recall times when I used to wonder what death would feel like. Maybe if I took my life, I wouldn't have to feel the pain over and over again. No one deserves the unbearable pains I endured, especially not me. I am the woman he stood before God with and exchanged vows—for better or worse. Well, I was at my worst…my breaking point…the point of no return.

I presented a barrage of questions again: God, why ME? Do you even hear me, God? How can You allow these things to happen to Your daughter? Is this my punishment for living a "worldly lifestyle" before marriage? Why is this happening to ME? Why, God? Do you see what is going on here? I felt like I was literally a doormat that this man kept stepping on!

People often ask me, *"Why did you stay?"* I stayed because he was my husband. He will change one day. He will stop drinking. We will be one big happy family again.

Sadly, the only changes I saw lasted every bit of three months. Then, we were right back to square one.

I became angry, upset all the time, and had panic attack after panic attack—only to find myself in the therapist's office. Mrs. "I got it…I can save the world…next time it will be different" needed someone to tell me whether or not I was the issue causing all of these problems. No answers came as to why my life looked like it could make the marquee for a Lifetime movie titled *"The Perfect Husband."*

After many years of the abuse, I then became very verbally abusive. What other weapons could I use to fight him with other than my tongue? I learned the hard way that my attempts at retaliating only served to make things worse. The more I cussed at, degraded, and said hurtful things to him, the more I suffered—to the point that I was running to the therapist's office like it was the grocery store! That became my temporary fix. I had someone who would listen to me, enabling me to feel like I had enough power to become whole again…if only for a moment. I had nervous breakdowns, became addicted to prescription medication, and slowly lost everything I had built from the ground up. Why should I care anymore? The one person I wanted more than anything treated me like I was nothing.

The day my husband said he wanted to be single and told me how my body looked disgusting to him was the day I knew he was just like every other man who hurt, abused and mistreated me. I saw the signs, though. I was witness to how badly he treated women before we got married. I even saw how he and his mother had a love/hate relationship, but I thought I was different. I just knew I was going to be the game-changer! If anything, the other women weren't worthy of having a man like him. As for me, I knew who I was and how much of an impact I had on others.

Again, I was wrong. I had to come to realize that people have to want to change. We can't go around thinking we can change the next person because we will end up hurt every time.

I started to analyze everything. I remembered that he said I looked disgusting to him, so I decided to "fix it." I went to doctor after doctor, trying to start every weight-loss plan there was — only for him not to notice my change. As time went on, I went from making a six-figure salary to sleeping on someone's couch with just a few clothes in a bag and my laptop. I had no money, no plan, and nowhere else to go. The only thing that made sense at the time was taking my prescription meds back to back to numb the pain so that I wouldn't have to think.

I told lie after lie to my family to cover up what I was really dealing with.

I told God at that moment that if **HE** made me well, I would never turn back. Well, God was gracious to me. I was made well and went back to a life that seemed 'normal.'

As if my husband were my 'god,' I quit praying when things were going well—and went running to the altar on Sunday when he didn't come home the night before. I was growing tired of living like that. On social media, I lived a happy life. In reality, I cried my eyes out every night and asked God to fix my husband. What I should have really been asking God to do was fix **ME**, clear away anything that blocked my vision, and remove the noise in the background. It was as if I was addicted to the pain I was receiving, all because I wanted his body next to me at night. I settled for a bedmate versus a soulmate. It didn't matter what happened or who he was with, as long as he turned that key in **OUR** door every night. Clearly, I didn't know my worth. I was selling my soul to the devil for a bed-filler. I didn't wait on a word from God because my mind was so cloudy.

Then, one day, I was sitting in my back yard and started talking to God. I asked Him, *"God, why ME?"* His response came through loud and clear:

"Why NOT you?"

It wasn't until years later—after the abuse, after him filing for divorce, and after he left me broke with no money to care for the kids and me—that I found purpose in my pain. I remember talking to a coworker one day during our lunch break, and she said that she was miserable and hated going home. She explained how her husband was verbally, physically, mentally, financially, and emotionally abusive. I asked her, *"Why are you staying?"* He response was matter-of-fact: *"I've been married to him for 20 years, and the abuse has been ongoing for the entirety of our marriage."* That woman sat in my car feeling hopeless after sharing her story with me. The look on her face gave me all the reason I needed.

She was my inspiration. I couldn't begin to imagine giving Mr. Perfect 20 years of my life without him changing. At that moment, with the bare minimum of everything, I didn't care about the house, Mercedes, trips around the world, sex, or shopping sprees. My healing and peace of mind were worth far more than any of those things. As much as it hurt, I knew that one day, I would be the woman who shared her story with other women who may be going through what I was choosing to leave behind.

My last conversation with my husband wasn't the best, but I finally used my voice and resolved to fight with everything inside of me—even if it meant death. I told him that me loving him was killing me and I could no longer be his lifeline. I had to save ME and be there to finish raising my kids, even if it meant me starting over and working in Corporate America until I built back up my businesses.

I started living for an audience of one. God was my Source and Provider. No matter how hard I fell, He made sure

I got back up so that I could pull up the next broken woman. I went from making six figures to losing everything, sleeping on a complete stranger's sofa, and catching rides. However, my peace was necessary. I had to go through the process. I lost it all, but the God I serve makes up the difference.

Four years later, God has **BLESSED** me with more than I could have ever imagined.

When life gets rough, stay on the course. No matter what the other person does to you, make sure you do your part to maintain your peace. Love should never hurt, and if he loves you, he would **NEVER** abuse you.

Dear God, thank *YOU* for choosing **ME**!

Discussion Questions

1. What does a "normal" day look like to you?

2. If there was one thing you could change about your present circumstances, what would it be and why?

Shade: No More Pain

Dewana Munoz

"There are no secrets that time does not reveal."
~ **Jean Racine** ~

THE SECRETS I HELD WITHIN

Growing up as a young girl, I always believed in love and finding that "someone special" to share my life with someday. I envisioned meeting that special one, feeling loved and protected.

Not once did I ever think I would become a victim of any type of abuse, be it physical, mental, or sexual.

As a child, I never experienced sexual or physical abuse. I did not know a thing about either because I neither saw nor heard any of the adults in my family talk about them. In my era, people simply did not speak about things of that nature around children. As a matter of fact, children were told to leave the room when grown folks were present and needed to have an "adult conversation." We rarely watched television in the late afternoons when the adult shows were on. When we did watch television, it was tuned to cartoons or educational programs.

In my family, we were taught to love one another, even our enemies. During weekly Bible studies, my mother taught us how to respect one another. She would place a particular emphasis on our ages — oldest to youngest — and that's how she would sit and line us up. My younger brothers were taught to respect women, starting with the women in our family. Respect was always essential in my household and was regularly driven into our brain. My mother stressed things like, *"The oldest gets to sit in the front seat"* and *"The oldest gets the first choice in everything."*

Domestic and sexual abuse were rarely openly addressed back in my day, as there wasn't a lot of information.

Dare to mention the word "sex" in my family, and there would be trouble! I never even thought about sex until I met my boyfriend, but what little I knew from viewing any form of intimacy was limited to seeing a couple either lying in bed kissing or simply holding hands. My family was devoted to loving Jehovah God and strictly abided by the teachings of the Bible. To that end, having an understanding of domestic violence left the question, *"What is **THAT**?"*, hanging in the air.

Often, I was alone and had no one to talk to about what was happening to me because everyone else worked in my family. I thought, *"Oh, my God! Who do I tell about what was happening to me? Who's going to believe me? God forbid I get him in trouble!"* That's all I kept thinking as I endured the emotional trauma and physical abuse.

Yes, you read correctly: I thought more of my abuser's safety than my own. That thing called "LOVE" had a certain kind of hold on me, leaving me to feel the need to protect him. My family knew nothing about what I was going through. I was too embarrassed and ashamed to open up.

I was raised in a Christian home. My family was a God-fearing people who taught me good morals, as well as how men should treat women and vice-versa. I thought all people were taught the same thing. I learned the hard way that I was wrong—and the hard way it truly was. I was physically abused and controlled by my boyfriend.

"Not ME!" I thought. *"Not abused by the one I trust and tell my most intimate secrets to! What?! Who do I tell? God forbid I get him into trouble!"*

I was still trying to process what was happening to me — and why it was happening. He and I had met on our way home from a ball game as we rode along with a mutual friend. His name was "Lorenz," and he was my first serious relationship.

At the time, I was dating "David." He and I got along well, and he treated me just as good. As time went on, he kept insisting on us taking our relationship to the 'next level.' Every time he pressed me to have sex with him, my answer was always *"No."* I wasn't ready to engage in that type of behavior because I had been taught that sex was only for married people ever since I was around five years old. As such, my Christian upbringing that placed a high value on the sanctity of marriage and sex — and my conscience — would not let me go there with him. Besides, I knew nothing about sex!

Then, I met Lorenz. He often came to my house with friends. One time, he asked me to come outside to talk to him. I agreed, and the pursuit was on. He kept pursuing me until I finally gave him my number. We spoke on the phone every day after school. Not even a month later, he asked me to be his girlfriend, and I said *"Yes!"*

At first, we got along great. We were very open with each other and talked about all sorts of things. Lorenz let me know in no uncertain terms that he did not like school. He often got into trouble and spent a lot of time at home after being expelled from school. *(I did not find this out until we had been dating for almost a year.)* Soon, things began to change between us. He would do things like show up at my house unannounced, and he grew very possessive.

One Monday morning before school, some friends and I were outside practicing for a competition in front of the school...and Lorenz showed up unexpectedly. He asked me to ride with him to grab a bite to eat for breakfast. Well, the bell was getting ready to ring in three minutes, so I told him *"No. I'm going to class. I'll talk to you later."* I found it strange that he showed up out of the blue. As he drove away, I heard him call me out of my name followed by a few choice words. I didn't believe it at first, but it was definitely him! From that day forward, he started trying to control me. Everywhere I went, he had to know who I was with and what time I would return. He also began to dictate what I could wear, the way I could sit, and the food I ate. I knew something was wrong here. Anytime someone would force their will on a teenager (or even an adult), that's wrong!

There were so many incidents that occurred during the seven years we dated. Lorenz was very demanding and persistent. After dating for about seven months, he started asking me to have sexual relations with him. Every time he brought up the subject, I would remind him I wasn't ready and talk about something else. I explained to him that I was waiting to get married and that I am a Christian girl, so *"No!"* was always my answer...until he kept pressing the issue.

Now, I had been taught a lot of things about relationships, but I was blindsided when it came to knowing how to handle a boy (or man) taking advantage of me. As such, I was powerless when it came to understanding males. Two years pass, and Lorenz always went out with his friends. If I wanted to do the same, it was a problem—especially if he didn't know where I was.

One Friday night, I went out with some friends of ours. We were sitting outside of the club on the top of the hood of my friend's car. Lorenz pulled up right in front of us and flashed his headlights in my face. I sat there and did not move, while he sat in his car for about five minutes loudly playing his music. When he finally got out of the car, he walked over to me and asked what I was doing sitting in the club's parking lot. He then grabbed me off the hood, pulled me to his car, and locked me inside. I repeatedly asked him to let me out while crying hysterically. Lorenz drove across the parking lot and stopped to talk to a friend. All the while, I was still locked inside of his car with the loud music. No one could hear my cries. Once he got back into the car, I again asked him to take me to my friend's house or drop me off at home. He refused and kept driving while I cried my heart out. **"Why is this happening to me?"** I thought.

For hours, I cried and cried until I fell asleep. The next day, he dropped me off at my friend's house. Why he did that, I had no clue. At this point, he was starting to scare me. I was shocked by what he did to me! Who could I tell about my fear without getting him into trouble — or worse yet, judge me? That was one of the first of many incidents to follow.

When we were in 10th grade, Lorenz was suspended (as usual) from school. He asked if he could see me, so I went over to his house. No one else was there. It was just Lorenz and me. He made a pallet on the floor, and we sat down and talked about our day, school, and some things he had going on. Soon after we got comfortable, he asked me to take off my clothes. I kindly told him, *"No. I'm a virgin and want to keep it that way."* The back and forth went on for about 30 minutes or so with him insisting that I get undressed. I then said, *"No. You are scaring me. I'm ready to go home now."* He tried talking me into staying and getting naked. His advances grew stronger and stronger, so I went to the bathroom in hopes that things would calm down in my absence. Instead, he followed me and told me how much he cared about me. I asked him, *"If you care, why are you asking me to do those things? I'm uncomfortable."* He replied, *"Because I love you. You are my girlfriend and one day, we will get married."* His response didn't ease my fear. He kept insisting that I take off my pants. When he got tired of begging, he forced himself on me. All the while, I was shaking and nervous. The experience was very uncomfortable, to say the least.

Right after that sexual encounter, Lorenz became obsessed with me. I recall one time, I was visiting his relative, and I asked her if I could practice driving her car up and down the street. She agreed to my request. No more than 15 minutes later, Lorenz showed up. He looked irritated as he parked his car. He then jumped out and yelled, **"What are you doing?"** He took the keys out of the ignition and asked, *"Who told you to drive?"* My reply was, **"I did!"** He stormed into his relative's house and asked her why she gave me her keys. They started arguing like cats and dogs. The next thing I heard was pictures falling off her wall from them fighting. They fought all the way to the bathroom, where they broke her sink.

Up to that point, I had never witnessed such violence before. I was again shocked and kind of scared of Lorenz because if he could fight with her over me, I just knew I was next.

I was 18 years old at the time. Some of our friends and his relative knew how abusive Lorenz was getting towards me.

I never told my mother because she was going through something of her own at home with my stepfather. I did not want to bother her with my "situation." Most times, I just figured out things on my own. I suffered in silence out of fear and shame. I didn't want to disappoint my family, so I stayed silent.

One morning, I woke up feeling sick. I vomited a green, slimy substance. I was scared and called out to my mother that I felt like I was dying. She took me to see my doctor. The doctor ran several tests on me. The nurse looked at me and said, *"You are not dying; however, you are going to be a mother."* I was shocked, scared, and confused at the same time. My life flashed before my eyes. **"Oh, no! Not another 18 years with that abusive man!"** I thought. (He and I had just broken up a month and a half before and I heard he had already started seeing someone new.) Before finding out I was expecting, I knew I wanted to be a mother someday, but not that soon. At 20 years old, I wasn't ready to be a mother—especially with someone who was not my husband and who was abusive and controlling.

I didn't want to tell him about the pregnancy. As a matter of fact, I wanted nothing at all to do with him, but my mother convinced me to call him to let him know I was pregnant. It was the hardest phone call I have ever made. Lorenz was actually happy! A few years prior, he had asked me to have his baby, although I told him I wouldn't because I had plans for my life—and they did not include him. *(At the time, we were still in high school. We had no jobs and no money…and we were still full-time students. Most of the things that came out of Lorenz's mouth made no sense to me. How would we care for a child without money?)*

My mother was still clueless about the things Lorenz had done to me because I had never told her. My parents worked long hours all the time. My mother worked the night shift, and we were at school during the day, so I barely even saw her. Lorenz took me to my doctor's appointments, dropped me off, and would tell me he'll be back to pick me up. One day, I waited almost two hours for him. He never showed up, so I started walking home. No one was available at home to pick me up because they were at work. So, I walked all the way home from the doctor's office. About five miles into my trip home, I stopped at a washeteria to catch my breath. I was so tired. I sat there for about 20 minutes before continuing on my way.

Lorenz was not active at all. I had to do everything on my own. When I was five months pregnant, I found out that another young lady lived in the house with Lorenz and his family. Her name was "Mandy." The whole time I was visiting, Mandy would walk around the house half-naked. I found that to be a little odd, considering we were all there. She wasn't friendly at all. She barely said a word to me. When Lorenz took me shopping and Mandy rode with us, she always seemed irritated by the idea of him shopping for and taking care of me. One day, Lorenz left for work, leaving Mandy and me alone in the house. Mandy kept making smart remarks to me. Every time I spoke, she would speak. Things quickly escalated. We started arguing and then she charged at me while I was sitting on the couch.

I was on the phone at the time, but I knew I had to fight her. I was tired and pregnant but fought as if I wasn't. I managed to get away from her and went across the street to a neighbor's house. I fell asleep and awoke the next morning around 6:00 a.m. When I went back to the apartment, Lorenz opened the door and asked me where I had been. He started arguing with me and asked, *"Why were you fighting Mandy while you are pregnant?"* He pulled me into the closet and started beating on me like a champion fighter. All that repeated in my head was, **"I need to protect my unborn baby!"** Later that day, Lorenz took me home. I felt sick, vomited everywhere, and then fell asleep.

Four months later, I gave birth to a healthy baby boy. I always knew Lorenz wasn't meant to be my husband because he was not the one designed just for me. We officially broke up when my son turned two years old. By that time, I had enough. He found someone else, and the rest is history! The break-up provided a sense of relief—as if weights had finally been lifted off my shoulders.

Looking back, I would tell my younger self that it's okay to love someone, but not at the expense of myself. Do not be ashamed of what happened. Speak up. Say something. You are not alone in this battle or cycle of abuse, be it sexual, mental, or physical. Better yet, call the police! Seek some help. Tell someone—your parents, teacher, counselor, pastor, aunt, uncle, whomever!

Listen: Do not be ashamed or embarrassed by what others think because so many women do not make it out of abusive situations alive. I was fortunate. I made it out and am glad to be here today sharing my journey with others with the hope that it will help someone else going through any type of abuse.

#DoNotStaySilentSpeakUp

Discussion Questions:

1. Why do you think the author of this story held so much in?

2. Do you think the author stayed with Lorenz too long? Why or why not?

3. What lesson(s) have you learned from this author's story?

Shade: No More Pain

Katrina Garrett

*"Never drown or lose consciousness
trying to save someone else."*
~ **Katrina Garrett** ~

UNCONSCIOUSLY SILENCED

Have you ever felt as if you were drowning, fighting to hang on for dear life? Have you ever felt trapped with no way out? As for me, I once lost myself in the process. In the beginning, I was beautifully blinded by my desire to feel wanted without caring for the consequences that were sure to follow that desire. I found myself confusing my choices. Did I crave being *wanted* or was I aching to be *loved*?

Sexual and lustful desires filled me in ways I hoped would fill the voids I did not know existed. I never really knew how to be alone. I was always used to having someone in my life. Whatever "he" came with, I thought I was ready for it all, but at the same time, I honestly didn't care because I was only seeking temporary satisfaction and gratification.

A few weeks after crossing paths with whom I will label a "beautiful disaster," I began to settle for everything—including the marriage I was tainting. All the signs were there from the beginning: jealousy, rage, overprotection, manipulation, and indescribable looks I could not quite understand. I mean, no one could even look my way or compliment me in any way. I purposely ignored those signs because I have always believed anyone could be fixed.

As time passed, we moved in with each other. Slowly, I began to drift away from family and friends—all because I thought I was happy. After living together for a few months, he convinced me to move to a new city that was more in his comfort zone. I found a good-paying job there and didn't mind the change of scenery. *(At the time, I had not considered the consequences of relocating, including losing my best friend. No family. No friends. No one but my child and him.)* A few months into adjusting to life in the new city, I began to feel a little uneasy. *Was my subconscious speaking to me?*

I now realize the uneasiness came from me trying to build a house on an unfinished foundation.

One evening, we had an argument. At the time, I had on a long white sundress and was sitting in a computer chair. He was sitting in front of me. The argument went much further than I had expected, causing me to mumble something in response to his last statement. With a look full of wrath, he firmly stated, **"Say it again!"** Not one to back down from an obvious dare, I began to boldly repeat what I said. Before I could complete my sentence, he punched me in my jaw! I fell to the floor. My eyes instantly filled with tears, as blood dripped from my mouth and onto my white dress. The next day, all I could do was stare at the swollen right side of my face in the mirror and question who I had become. The slightest attempt at smiling pained me. He later apologized, and we both acted as if the incident never happened.

I had no idea that it was just the beginning of what was to come.

The verbal abuse, emotional abuse, physical abuse, and cheating began to happen more frequently. They became so commonplace, to the point of me knowing when and what to expect from him.

The next time he **physically** abused me, we had been in an argument about him cheating on me. He flipped over the refrigerator and trashed the entire house. He then threw me on the couch and held me down by my neck while trying to force a dog biscuit into my mouth. As I looked into his eyes, I could see anger, hatred…and hurt.

After church one evening, another disagreement transpired. During this incident, he poured bleach on me and my clothes in the closet, and he broke my phone. I had bleach dripping from the tip of my head to the soles of my feet. As I sat in the tub to cleanse myself from the stench and burn of the chemical, I just cried. I kept repeating in my head *"Why?"* It seemed that things turned from bad to worse in a relatively short amount of time. I found myself building up the courage to leave, but I always went back to him. I never really knew why I went back; I just did.

When I found out that I was pregnant with my middle child, the abuse was much worse than it had been in the beginning. A few days after I was released from the hospital from giving birth to my son, he stomped on me until I vomited. I was very sick because I had caught an infection after giving birth and was in a fragile condition. As a result of the constant abuse and toxicity of the relationship, I began to lose weight due to stress and depression.

After the birth of my son, we moved to another city farther away from what was familiar to me. I sent my children to live with my mother and sister. *It did not seem like it at the time, but sending them away was the hardest thing I could have ever done as a mother.* In this new city, I caught this man and a very close friend of mine having sex. It all felt like a bad dream—one that I was fighting to wake up from to make it all disappear. However, the reality was that it **wasn't** a bad dream. Around this same time, I was sneaking to talk to my best friend, whom

I had lost at the beginning of this relationship. When 'Mr. Cheater' found out I was talking to him, he grabbed me by my ponytail and banged my head against the cement stairs. I was pulling back and trying to break free, but he wouldn't let me go. No matter how hard I tried, I could not get loose from his grip.

It was at this time in the relationship that I had lost myself. I did not know who I was anymore. It was as if I was just existing on Earth; not really **LIVING**. Well, I ended up leaving him again and moved back to my hometown.

NOTE: Only *YOU* know when you have had enough. Only *YOU* know how much more you can take.

As fate would have it, I was not yet fed up with his foolishness. Something kept me tied to this man, and it felt as though I could not break free.

Maybe it was the soul tie.

Maybe it was because of the children.

Maybe it was because I did not want to be alone.

Maybe it was his skilled, manipulative ways.

Not even a few months later, I was back to visiting him. Soon after, I moved back in. I then became pregnant with my daughter. During this time, the physical abuse had tapered off a bit, but the emotional and verbal abuses were ongoing.

One day, I received a call from him while I was at work. He instructed me to come home because there was a lady who had stopped by to speak with me. He provided me with the woman's number, and I called her on my way home. The lady worked for Child Protective Services (CPS). I allowed her to return to my home so that we could talk. As I stood in my living room, she informed me that someone "anonymously" reported to CPS that my children were being abused, prompting an investigation. Not thinking clearly, I became very aggressive towards her. I just stared at my children's father in such an unforgiving way because I knew deep down inside it was one of the women he had been cheating with who called CPS to my home. Before the investigator came to my house, I learned she had already visited the daycare my children attended and evaluated them. All this time, as the investigator was talking to me, I could see that her mouth was moving, but I wasn't hearing a thing she was saying.

I had never felt so empty. I had never experienced so much pain in my entire life.

On a different occasion, the rage had grown so strong, I called the police out to our home. The officers informed me that because we were both on the lease, they could not **make** him leave. So, I took my children and went to a friend's house. As I was getting in the car and as he sat handcuffed on the porch with the police standing around him, he said, *"You better not leave. If you leave, you will regret it."* I ignored him and left anyway. He knew I only had one friend who lived in the city, so after a few hours of being at my friend's place, he came on his motorcycle and rode through her apartment complex while screaming my name. The kids began to get a little noisy, so we sat in a closet until we all fell asleep. As I laid in the closet with my babies, I didn't know what to think. I was scared to go back home—but did so the next morning.

That morning, I sat in my car as he watched me through the open front door. Eventually, he walked over to the car, told me to get out, and assured me he wasn't going to do anything to me. I was hesitant at first but decided to get out of the car, go inside the house, and get dressed for work. From that day forward, I continued to go to work with a smile on my face. No one knew all that was hiding behind that smile. It was masking embarrassment, brokenness, hurt, pain, sorrow, unforgiveness, silent cries, hushed screams for help, confusion, loneliness, emptiness, and so much more.

The arguments between him and I became predictive, and the apologies lost their sincerity. Over time, I began to study and learn his ways a little more. When I knew our conversations were headed in the wrong direction, I used to put my babies in the playroom and close the door because I did not want them to see their daddy and me in any type of commotion. There was a time when I had tired of allowing him to hit on me and I fought back. After a while, fighting back didn't work. He ended up choking me until I lost consciousness. Choking me was his way of stopping me from fighting back.

One day, I told him that he had to leave and could not come back. He left with ease, but moreso because he had someone else in mind whom he could manipulate. After a while, it was just my babies and me. The nights became cold and lonely. It felt as though I was drowning in my own turmoil. I was bitter and had so much anger within me. He would send me text messages saying certain things that he would only know if he were actually in my presence at the time. I couldn't understand how he knew those things. I later found out he was stalking me in the uncomfortableness of my own home. Shortly after this revelation, I snuck and moved back to my hometown without telling anyone that I was leaving. I took my children out of daycare, packed our clothes, and left everything else behind. I finally had enough.

When I moved back home, it was at the top of my list to visit my best friend. He did not know I was coming back. After four long years of not communicating with him or my godchild, I made it my business to have a face-to-face conversation. All I wanted to do was sincerely apologize to him for damaging our friendship. I wanted him to forgive me for the pain I had caused him during my four-year absence. I never had anyone accept me the way my best friend did. Despite the pain I had put him through, and although I felt like I had lost him. He forgave me and accepted me back with open arms like we never missed a day. His genuine and pure love for me never changed. Today, we have been best friends for 14 years and counting. Our bond is bittersweet.

During the initial phase of my separation from my abuser, I was bitter and had become rather beastly. I had fallen into a depressive state and was prescribed medication. I cried every single day for months. The medication numbed my feelings, leaving me feeling trapped in my own body and silently crying out for help. I hated the way the drug made me feel, so I flushed all of them down the toilet. It was then I began to know God for myself. I never had a close relationship with Him, but knew I had to find a way to break free once and for all. I started having daily "meetings" with God, giving Him *HIS* just-due time in my life.

Oh! I can't forget to mention here: God led me to genuinely forgive the close friend I have known since elementary school—the one who had sex with my children's father. We are closer now than we were in the past. God healed my heart and mended what was broken within our friendship.

Often, we don't know how to forgive, or we simply make a choice not to forgive. We allow our emotions to choose our path, not knowing that our emotions can lead us to destruction. It is then that bitterness comes knocking and we accept that emotion with open arms. We then begin to carry that baggage full of burdens—ones we do not have to bear. It's important to understand the vicious cycle of unforgiveness:

- Pain leads to damage.
- Damage leads to brokenness.
- Brokenness leads to unforgiveness.

Be encouraged: **Brokenness can be mended!** Don't allow unforgiveness to weaken you. You are much stronger than you give yourself credit for. Heal! Peace is knocking on your door!

Why I left is far more important than why I stayed. I had to find the courage to understand why I didn't stay. No one could decide for me; I had to know my 'whys.' I had to overcome the fear of leaving.

Many people judge from the outside looking in, not knowing all that is truly going on nor the battles that you may be fighting mentally, physically, spiritually, and emotionally. People are so curious to know, *"Why did you stay?"*, but they are unaware of the unconscious drowning that occurs with no visible lifeguard in sight.

As I reflect, I now know my story was being told through my silence…*but who was really listening?*

The silence of your scream can be dangerous. Sometimes it may seem like the louder you scream, the quieter you become. You are crying out, yet no one hears you. You feel as if you're being buried alive, suffocating in your pain, hurt, betrayal, challenges, and disappointments. You believe no one would understand. I know. I've been there.

Today, I am **FREE**! You have the opportunity to be **FREE** as well! Will you take that leap of faith for your sanity and the safety of your children?

Discussion Questions

1. Do you know who you are? Explain in detail who you believe you are today and who you desire to become.

2. Have you ever lost yourself in "the process"? What did that 'look' like? How did you overcome?

Shade: No More Pain

Tosha R. Dearbone

"Sometimes, it's better to keep silent than to tell others what you feel because it will only hurt you when you know they can hear you but don't understand."
~ Author Unknown ~

Tosha R. Dearbone

TOO SILENT TO BE HEARD

I wish I had known when I was younger that speaking up may have given me peace of mind a lot sooner. I am now in my 30s and have finally found my voice.

You see, I did not **know** I was being sexually abused at the tender age of seven. One day, I was at my dad's house, and my cousin was visiting. My dad said he would be right back and left to go to the store, leaving me alone with my cousin. I remember coming out of the restroom and walking into the living room where he was lying on the couch watching television. I can also recall him rubbing his genitals and then asking me to touch him there. Even at the age of seven, I knew in my mind something wasn't right with his request, but I trusted him and believed he would never do anything to hurt me. So, I proceeded with his request. I didn't tell my dad what my cousin had me do because he pleaded with me not to say anything.

Some years passed, and I recall playing a game called "House." "House" was a childhood game involving one person playing the mother and the other filling the role of the father. As a couple, there was kissing and feeling on each other, truly acting like husband and wife. Everyone I knew played the game.

Well, one day, I was visiting a friend, and she wanted to play "House." She locked her bedroom door because her brothers were home at the time. She stated that she would be the mother and me, the father. She laid me down on her bed and kissed me, touched my breasts, and proceeded to rub my vagina. Again, I knew it was wrong, but how would I be able to explain what we were doing to anyone? She and I participated in this behavior every time I visited. I was so confused (**Satan** *is the author of confusion*). I know you're probably thinking, *"Well, did you think you were gay at the time?"* My answer is no; I didn't. I acknowledge the awkwardness of the situation but did not know who to tell. I felt like if I said something, no one would believe me. I was kept bondage to that silence. I eventually stopped visiting my 'friend.' I did not explain; I just abruptly ceased going there. Plus, I had switched schools and made new friends.

Then, at the age of 15, while I was asleep in my bed, I heard a voice in the middle of the night say, *"Have you ever been touched like this before?"* I immediately opened my eyes to find my brother's friend kneeled at my bedside with one hand on my thigh and the other rubbing my breast. Shocked, I asked him, **"What are you doing? Why are you in here?"** He paused and replied, *"Oh, no! Please don't tell your brothers. They will kill me!"* He hurried to get up and quickly left my room. That incident left me feeling scared and confused. **Why did these things keep happening to me?**

Meanwhile, I was still under the impression that if I told anyone, my family would suffer behind what was happening to me. Surely, someone would end up in jail or get hurt. So, I never told.

As time progressed, I tried to block out the instances of sexual abuse from my memory. I then found myself entering another level of abuse: physical.

I started dating my first child's father in middle school. At the age of 16, we had a baby. He was a good guy but had cheating ways—and I always found out. On one particular day, we were arguing, and I remember him grabbing my arm. When he did that, I instantly went into react-mode, grabbed his hand, and twisted it...**HARD**! I never envisioned him being violent with me in any way. After all, we had known each other for so long and had our first child together. Violence was **never** an issue before. I suppose you never really know a person until you catch them doing something they did not want you to find out about. We ended up separating—and I went on with my life as a single teenage mother.

Six months later, I transferred schools. I met a new guy, and we started kicking it together. It must be noted here that my mom and I often argued, leaving me to choose to do things my way. Well, not long after this new guy and I started dating, things started moving fast. We decided to move in together and live as a family. Things were so crazy between us because he was a 'street boy.' He ran the streets, sold drugs, and was a promiscuous liar. Things began to take a turn for the worse, and I felt the environment was unsafe for my daughter and me.

We moved out and back home with my mom *(something I honestly did* **NOT** *want to have to do)*. Instantly, I replayed the verbally abusive words spoken by my family:

> *"You ain't nothing but a ho."*

> *"You think you're holier than thou."*

> *"You're not good enough."*

I despised the way I was made to feel and had not one single person to talk to about it. I tried to remain focused, stay in school, work, and raise my child, but it was hard living somewhere where I felt like an outsider.

At that moment, I realized I was missing my dad. He had passed away shortly after I was sexually abused at his apartment. At times, I wanted to reach out to my mom, but our relationship was not open to discussions such as the ones I needed. As for my brothers, they treated me as if we weren't even related. I felt so alone. Strangely enough, I wasn't a bad child by no means. I was the atypical teenager who wanted to grow up fast, with my 'teachers' being my friends on "the streets."

I can recall having a conversation with my mom about me getting my own apartment. I don't know how we got on the subject, though. To my surprise, she said yes! I was a tad bit scared but definitely excited about her approval! So, at the age of 16 and with a child, I was living on my own and doing better than some adults were (in my opinion). I was still working and going to school...and then decided to get back with my last boyfriend. Why, you ask? Because I felt I **needed** to be with someone. Plus, he continued to feed me that famous line: *"It will not happen again."*

For a while, things were going great—even though he was still "doing him." Almost two years into this toxic relationship, my confidence had grown, and I started telling myself, *"I can do this alone! I don't need to be in this type of relationship!"* Right when I was ready to get my breakthrough, those thoughts came back and slapped me in the face when I started to feel sickly. I visited the doctor the next day or so, and the doctor said, *"Ma'am, you're pregnant."* My heart dropped— not because I was pregnant but because I felt trapped in an ongoing problem that seemed would **NEVER** get any better. When I told him I was pregnant, he was happy and began treating me with a little respect.

One night, I received a phone call that started like this:

"Harris County Jail. Will you accept the charges?"

Instantly, I felt a new level of rage overcome me. I accepted the call. It was him on the other end, assuring me that he was coming home soon and not to worry *(he came back a few days later)*. What I did not know at the time was that him being in and out of jail was going to be my new norm. However, his constant absence, raising my daughter alone, the pregnancy, and the alarming emotional abuse had taken its toll on me.

During one of his "out of jail" times, he came to the apartment we shared with a female in my car. *(I guess he thought I wouldn't get up to look outside – but I did.)* Immediately, I started asking questions. **"Who is she? Why do you have her in my car?"** He replied, *"Girl, you're tripping! She ain't nobody."* I persisted with the questioning. He then pulled out a gun, put it to my head, and hollered, **"Girl, I will kill you!"** Out of fear and finally fed up, my response came back with the sharpness of a sword: *"You can do whatever you think is best!"* He must have seen the craziness in my eyes because he laughed and then left – but not before saying aloud, **"This girl is crazy!"**

You may be shocked to learn I continued with this toxic relationship for a couple more years, off and on. A majority of his time away from home was spent in jail. Not long after delivering my second child, we parted ways once and for all.

I soon began to find me. I started to see who I was and what I liked. Although you may find this difficult to believe, my relationship with Christ grew stronger as well. I truly loved the new me!

In 2003, I decided to start dating again. As I reflect on this time in my life, I guess I can admit I was attempting to fill a void. I met this new man in a nightclub, and we started kicking it right away. He was a cool guy and fun to be around. There was one major flaw: He was a female magnet, too! He would lie with ease and tell me females were his sisters. By the time the truth came out, wouldn't you know? I had gotten myself into another "situation." I was pregnant again! *Why, Lord? Why do I keep putting myself in situations where I end up pregnant, in an unhealthy relationship, and left feeling hurt and alone?* As my life would have it, my unborn child's father quickly showed me he had no intention of being there for our child and that he was not going to stop cheating on me.

I became so deeply hurt and confused. My life from the age of seven to 24 years old looked dark and bleak. No one could tell me there wasn't a black cloud hovering over me. Once again, I contemplated committing suicide—reminding me of the time I swallowed an entire bottle of Tylenol (over 50 pills) at the age of 16. Obviously, nothing tragic happened to me, but the act of following through let me know I could have control over something…especially my life.

Around the middle of 2004, I started working at a group home facility. I was very proud of myself! I did not allow my past to keep me down. Instead, I used it to propel me forward to being one of my own biggest motivators! I completed homeschooling to obtain my high school diploma, worked hard to receive my certification as a Medical Assistant, started a new job, and raised three children on my own. I was well on my way to **FINALLY** getting into the rhythm of fulfilling my dreams.

Everything was going great for me, so I decided to try dating again. I met this guy who was fun to be around. He and I could talk about anything. We instantly hit it off and decided to become a couple. The first year of our relationship was what I had always envisioned when it came to enjoying life with a mate. We got an apartment and were doing great! Then (as was customary for my life), things begin to take a turn for the worse.

His child's mother started making three-way calls to him while I was on the other line. He didn't know I was listening in on their conversations. He would tell me he was at work when, in actuality, he was on his way to visit her.

I fell into that familiar place again: feeling low and back into the same situation I just got out of a year prior. *What was I doing wrong?* I prayed and continued to weigh my options: Should I go back to my mom's house or stay in the situation?

I chose to stay.

Months passed by, and nothing whatsoever changed. He was still lying and cheating (something he vehemently denied doing).

One evening, we got into it really bad. I cannot recall the exact conversation at this moment, but I can remember the blow to my head and him pulling my hair. I snapped! All I could think of at the moment was that the abusive cycle I found myself in had to come to a **STOP!** I ran into the kitchen and grabbed a butcher knife. I was out of my mind to the point of no return. As he went to grab it away from me, I swung. The blade cut him from one end of his hand to the other. I immediately called the police. When they arrived, they asked him if he wanted to press charges. He refused. Another officer asked me the same question, and I declined. However, they did make him leave. I remember feeling both bad for him and grateful at the same time. The abuse was over! With him gone, my mind was made up. It was time to go. I packed up my children's and my things over the next couple of days and moved back home with my mom.

Once settled, I sat in the room and repeatedly asked myself, *"How did I ever get on this path of abuse and not loving myself enough that I continued to gravitate towards men who treated me with no respect?"* All that came back in response was silence. I had **no** answers.

Moving forward, I was determined to get myself back on track. My focus was on my children, work, and anything that kept me from feeling depressed. After living with my mom for six months, I found a house, and my children and I moved. I was definitely back on the rhythm of finding me again.

Some years went by, and I did date again; however, unlike before, at the **first** indication that the relationship was unhealthy, I ended it. Was I lonely? At times, yes. What I came to know was that I meant more to myself than to settle, be abused, or allow myself to be treated as if I didn't matter.

I remember my daughter saying to me, *"Momma, just be by yourself for a while."* To hear those words from my child, I knew I had to do something. I decided to remain single until

GOD sent me my mate. I would no longer put myself in those predicaments. I needed to learn how to love **ME**, and by doing so, that meant asking God to remove the desire of me needing to be with someone. God was my comfort; He was my peace. Now, don't get me wrong: I do want to consider marriage one day, but until then, I am good!

Even today, I tend to think back on my younger years and wonder where I went off track. I want to say it's because I saw and heard the abuse my mom and dad inflicted on each other, coupled with my brothers and their girlfriends having their abusive encounters. I grew up having no clue what a healthy relationship looked like until my stepdad came into my life (which was **after** the "damage" had been done during those critical influential years). My stepdad came to be one of my favorite people, despite the trials and judgments from my dad's side of the family. My stepdad would always tell me, *"Little Baby, you can do it!"* Those words are a constant reminder, even as I walk out this journey today. Now, I tell myself often that I am accepted, loved, and worthy of the utmost respect…and so are you!

Discussion Questions

1. When in **any** given "situation", do you feel it's best to speak up or not? Why or why not?

2. If you had the chance to look within, would you say you truly accept who you are? Describe here what you envision you would see inside your soul.

___
___
___
___
___
___
___
___
___
___
___
___
___
___
___
___
___
___
___
___

Shade: No More Pain

Tearini Hubert

"Know your worth so that you don't settle for anything less than what you deserve, Queen. Follow your instincts. When something isn't right, it's protecting you."
~ Tearini Hubert ~

Tosha R. Dearbone

BUT YOU LOVE ME, THOUGH...

Growing up, I'm sure many young girls dreamt about their "Prince Charming" who would come and sweep them off of their feet. There would be a beautiful wedding, ending with them riding off into the sunset on a horse-drawn carriage. I was no different.

From the very moment I met "Mike," there was something about him that swept me off my feet. I was like, *"Yasss! I want to be his woman!"* —and I was determined to be just that! When Mike and I started conversing, we didn't live in the same city limits. At the time, he was working in a different state. I remember talking to him every night until we fell asleep. The butterflies that flittered in my belly confirmed I had finally met my "Mr. Right."

Mike and I met through social media. I was fresh out of being released from a very toxic relationship with an older, crazy man. Honestly, I wasn't ready for a relationship; neither was I prepared to have sex with Mike, so him being in a different state didn't bother me. I let him know that I was celibate and wasn't trying to be somebody's "sex buddy." After talking for about a month, he stated he was going to try to make things work with his child's mother because *"he couldn't see himself being with someone who didn't want to put out"* [have sex]. My response was, **"Cool! I wish y'all the best!"** I then deleted his number and our message thread from my phone—and moved on with my life.

I didn't hear from Mike for months until right before the new year was about to start. At the time, I had already begun conversing with another man who was kind to both my two-year-old son and me. When Mike contacted me, I let him know about my new relationship and that my new man and I were planning on taking a trip the following month for my birthday. The first thing Mike was concerned about was whether or not my new man and I had sex. I was still practicing celibacy at that point, and it was nice not to be pressured by him about it. To be honest, he never even brought up sex in our conversations.

For the next few weeks, I started going out on dates with Mike — but also still going on dates with the other man as well. I didn't see anything wrong with it because neither of them were technically "my man." In my book, I was still single.

Right before my birthday, I ended up breaking my celibacy with Mike. I didn't see the trap. I didn't recognize the amount of attention he focused on me was all a part of his "plan." **Oh, how I should have paid closer attention to that first sign God showed me!** I ended up hurting the other man I was talking to. He warned me about Mike. He told me that all Mike wanted to do was have sex with me, not want me to mess around with another man (due to his fear of another man doing right by me), and that he didn't want anything more from me than sex.

From the time that Mike and I first had sex, we kept at it on and off for the next few years. Every time I told him I needed and deserved more than "just sex," he **ALWAYS** found something small to argue about so that he could leave and not talk to me for a few days. A few days would eventually turn into weeks; weeks turned into months—but he wouldn't go past two months without talking to or questioning me about what I was doing and who I was doing it with. This behavior became a predictable part of his routine. It was so typical, I would start talking to other dudes when he went off on his little "mad spree." When he would call after his tantrum, I always answered and gave up my goodies. Mike and I became so comfortable with each other that we started having unprotected sex.

It must be noted here that before I began practicing celibacy, I was tested for all sexually-transmitted diseases (STDs) and the results came back that I was clean.

I started noticing that Mike's phone would often ring when he and I were together, but he wouldn't answer the calls. I questioned him about it, and he would say, *"You're not my girlfriend. I don't owe you an explanation as to why I'm not answering MY phone."* All the while, I was still doing my little "side thing." The difference between Mike and I was that I was honest with him and whomever else I was conversing with.

Something told me that if he was hiding something in his phone, there's something else he's not telling me. My gut screamed, **"GO GET TESTED!"** I listened.

When my test results came back, they confirmed my suspicions: Mike had given me an STD! I was so hurt. How could he do me like that? He obviously didn't care about my health since he was having unprotected sex with other females, too. I questioned him and asked if he was having unprotected sex with anyone else. At first, he told me he wasn't. When I pressured him for the truth, he hesitated and then replied, *"Yeah, but it's only two or three other girls besides you."*

IT'S ONLY TWO OR THREE OTHER GIRLS BESIDES ME?!!!

Those are the words that kept running through my head. I didn't tell Mike I had received my test results back that day. I didn't tell him he had given me an STD. What I did tell him, however, was that he needed to get tested.

I got tired of being Mike's "sex buddy" whenever he wanted, while he jumped in and out of relationships with all of those different females. I was sick of his lies about them, too. I do accept my level of blame for allowing him to keep up that behavior for as long as he did without me putting my foot down. Eventually, I told him I couldn't do it anymore and that I was done with him for real this time. Why did I go and say that?

Supposedly, Mike really wanted to be in a committed relationship then, but I didn't. Still, I was so in love with him. What was a girl supposed to do? At the back of my mind, I really didn't want to be with him, but then again, he was the man I fell in love with and invested time and feelings into — so, why not?

Our relationship started out well. We went out on dates every other weekend, and I was happy…until the phone stuff started happening again. At one point, he cracked the screen on his phone, so I thought it was the perfect opportunity for him to get not only a new phone but also a new phone number. Much to my surprise, he agreed!

I never realized just how much he was forcing sex into our relationship until the day when I was dead tired after work and didn't want to do it. He actually got mad and had an attitude! I finally gave in, and we had sex. That would not be the last time he would force the issue of sex in our relationship.

I recall the day Mike and I got into it really bad about the phones (yet again). When he opened the front door, he slammed it into the wall and left a small hole. I was furious! I screamed, *"Bye! Leave and don't come back!"*

Within a few hours, we were back to talking to each other…again.

God kept showing me signs that Mike and I shouldn't have been together, but my "love" for Mike kept me from risking what he and I had built. Honestly, I didn't want to start over.

The controlling, manipulative, and narcissistic behavior grew progressively worse as the months passed. It got to a point where he was going through **MY** phone two or three times a week—that I **KNEW** about. There's no telling how many times he did that when I put it down somewhere or went to sleep. Mike's "curiosity" caused us to get into it because of the texts I sent to this guy I went to church with. This was the first time he put his hands on me. He read the messages and asked me why we were texting. I told him that we always chat and that it wasn't anything serious. My casual response angered him. He threw my phone down onto the carpet, and when I got up to retrieve it, he grabbed me by my face and pushed me. In my defense, my automatic response was to swing at him. When I did that, he tackled me onto the bed, pinned me down, and told me, ***"You better not EVER swing at me again in your LIFE!"*** I was ready to **FIGHT**, but he quickly got off of me, left out of the room, and slammed the door shut behind him as if he just spanked a child.

A few hours later, he came back and apologized. He promised he would never put his hands on me again and went on to explain that he got jealous of me texting another man who was obviously flirting with **HIS** woman. I didn't respond verbally; I just rolled my eyes at him.

The "never will happen again" happened the next month again — but that time, it was worse.

We went out to celebrate his friend's birthday and had been drinking and enjoying ourselves. I saw a local celebrity and wanted to speak to him. Mike pulled me by my arm out of the club. I was so embarrassed. We argued all the way to the car. When we got inside the car, he threatened to punch me in my face for acting like a whore in front of his friends. Me being who I am, I told him, *"You are **NOT** going to put your hands on me without a fight!"* (I grew up fighting with my brothers, so it was nothing for me to fight back.) As we drove away, I figured that if I just shut up, maybe he would do the same and calm down enough to concentrate on the road and stop swerving before we got pulled over by the cops.

When we pulled up to the house, he jumped out of the car, met me at the front door, and yelled, *"I was talking to you! You don't hear me talking to you?"* Before I had a chance to respond, he slapped me. We started fighting right then and there—right outside the house. (I don't recall how we stopped fighting.) I went inside, got my son, and brought him into the room with me. Mike came into the room, still trying to fight with me. I told him, *"I'm not about to fight you, and you are not going to fight me in front of my child!"* I went and woke up Mike's mother and told her to get her son because he was not going to keep putting his hands on me. If he did, one of us was going to end up in the hospital or a grave—and I guaranteed it wouldn't be me. As she and I walked out of the room, Mike ran up on me, and his mom had to intervene to get him off of and from around me. I went back into my room with my child, who was crying hysterically at this point. As I tried to calm down my child, Mike's mom came into the room and asked, *"What did you do to him to make him act like that?"*

I replied, *"Nothing. We went out, and both of us were drinking. He accused me of being a whore and then started tripping by trying to put his hands on me!"*

His mom even went so far as to ask if I wanted to leave for the night until he calmed down. I told her I didn't want to leave because it was late and that I didn't want to go to my parents' house at that time of the morning because they would question me about what happened. I didn't want my family involved in our business.

All that kept playing in my head repeatedly was, **"What did I do to him?"** Mike's mother couldn't keep out of the room, so she went and got Mike's little brother to help calm him down. His behavior scared my child. I called Mike's friend and told her that he had put his hands on me. She responded the same way Mike's mother did: *"What did you do to him?"*

WHAT DID I DO TO HIM??? Did I really do something to make him want to put his hands on me like that? Was it the way I talked to him that triggered him to explode? Did he feel disrespected because I wanted to speak to the local celebrity in the club? All of those questions ran through my mind, leaving me to feel like I really **DID** do something wrong.

I hung up the call and continued focusing on calming my child down and putting him back to sleep. I then called my best friend and told her what happened. She and her husband were furious about the abuse and the fact that he had tried to fight with me in front of my son. They had never seen Mike upset, so they had a hard time picturing him going "full-throttle" like that. In a matter of minutes, my friend and her husband came to my house. I went outside to talk to them as they comforted me. I needed to talk to someone who **DIDN'T** accuse me of being the cause of Mike's behavior and who understood my point of view. I stood outside and spoke to them for about an hour. That entire time, Mike's mother was watching us through the window…and stirring his pot of anger even more by telling him I called a man over to the house to fight him. I don't know why she said that to him, as I would never do such a thing. All I wanted Mike to do was leave me alone and get himself some help. I truly loved him!

When I went back into the house after talking to my friend and her husband, Mike was asleep on the couch. He was snoring and had a bottle of liquor lying next to him on the floor. Once I made it back upstairs and retrieved my phone, I had multiple messages from Mike telling me how sorry he was. He blamed his actions on the alcohol, promised he wouldn't do it again, begged me not to leave him, said he loved his family, and that he didn't mean it. I believed he really loved me and that he was truly sorry about what happened that night. What I didn't know was that his actions that night would change my life forever.

No longer do I look past the signs that are presented in a person when getting to know them and/or dating them. Neither do I second-guess myself and my woman's intuition when it tells me something isn't right about a person.

I now have an organization for young ladies and women to overcome all the obstacles that life throws at them. Together, we can be **VICTORIOUS**! I have learned that it's not always about the destination but rather about the *journey* that will actually lead us into our purpose!

Discussion Questions

1. Is it possible to genuinely love a narcissistic man like Mike? Why or why not?

2. If you've ever been in an abusive situation and left, what was it that gave you the strength to leave?

_____
_____
_____
_____
_____
_____
_____
_____
_____
_____
_____
_____
_____
_____
_____
_____
_____

3. How would you advise someone else who may be going through something similar to exit a toxic relationship?

_____
_____
_____
_____
_____
_____
_____
_____
_____
_____
_____
_____
_____
_____
_____
_____
_____
_____
_____

Tosha R. Dearbone

Shade: No More Pain

Reyna Harris-Goynes

"It was just a lesson, not a life sentence."
~ Author Unknown ~

Tosha R. Dearbone

IN THE MIDST OF IT ALL

For 14 years, on and off, I was in a relationship riddled with domestic violence. In the beginning, things were cool; however, as time progressed, my partner started to change. The man who would later become my "baby's daddy" was working and getting paid weekly at the time. With that money, he was supposed to help me with the bills. Instead, he helped his mom (whom I felt was taking advantage of the situation) because she was constantly telling him she needed money for "this and that"—although she received a regular monthly income! As time went on, there was one instance I recall when he got paid, and the latest Jordan's sneakers came out. He bought pairs for my sons and me but didn't have enough money to buy himself a pair. We got into an argument about that, and by the end, he had burned all three pairs.

While in the relationship, I found out he "supposedly" had a baby by another woman. After the mother filed for child support and the DNA test was performed, it was proven the baby wasn't his. He was upset about that situation because he really wanted that baby, but later down the line before our son was born (and while we were still together), he did father another child…that he denied.

During our relationship, I gave birth to a little girl. I could tell instantly that he was a bit jealous of her. For instance, we would go shopping at Wal-Mart often. Almost every time, if I had a little extra money, I would buy my daughter something. There was one particular time I bought her something, and he got angry because once we went through the check-out, he had to put his stuff back. When we arrived home, instead of taking his anger out on me, he picked up my son and hung him over the balcony of our apartment, threatening to drop him. Every single day, it was something different with him. He wanted everything to go his way or no way. If he didn't get his way, he acted like a spoiled child.

He said he wanted to marry me, but I refused to marry a liar, cheater, and manipulator all wrapped up into one. This man cheated on me the whole time we were together. When people would tell me what he was doing, he, of course, said they were lying.

I recall another instance when we got into it and, at the time, my daughter had some Mardi Gras beads tangled in her hair. Instead of him taking the time to untangle the beads, he pulled them out of her head — right along with her hair.

He had control of all the money, so there were times when my children and I went hungry while he went out to get himself something to eat. If I didn't answer my phone when he called the first time or when I hung up on him, he would call me back constantly until I answered. I had very few male friends because he didn't approve of those types of friendships, yet it was supposed to be okay for him to walk away from me while in a store (for example) to hold conversations with other women. When we were home, I knew he was conversing with other women because he would either go outside or into another room to talk on the phone. God forbid I did something like that! There would've been a war!

I felt like our whole relationship was built on lies, cheating, and unnecessary drama — which is too much for anyone to handle. I was often unhappy, severely depressed, and outright miserable. There were times when I didn't know whether I was coming or going. I was in a deep, dark place. Some days, I didn't even want to get out of the bed because I wanted to sleep all day or lay there and watch TV. I got to a point where I didn't want to be bothered by anyone—including family—because I didn't care about myself or anything else besides my children.

Eventually, I ended that relationship and started one with someone else. It didn't last for a few reasons, to include him cheating with other girls in my apartment complex as well as him listening to other things (lies) people said about me. My cousin—who acted like she couldn't stand him at all—was one of the people doing underhanded mess with him behind my back after he got out of jail. A few weeks before he went to jail, a friend of his was playing with a gun. At the time, I was sitting in front of them, and it just so happened the gun went off. I was able to quickly lean to the right as the bullet whizzed by my face and struck another friend in the leg. I was evicted the next day. It didn't help that the apartment manager lived right behind me. The guy who was playing with the gun couldn't even look at me in the face after that happened. *I still can't believe my children slept through the whole ordeal. They didn't budge—not even once.*

After that incident, I moved. Although I still had feelings for the other guy, I took my "baby's daddy" back. **Why did I do that?** The arguments and abuse began again almost immediately after he moved in with me. We argued a lot about him not having a job and not helping me pay bills. He said he quit his job so that he could stay at home with our daughter.

That went on for an entire year before I became fed up with not getting any help from him.

This same man tried to control my every move, especially when it came to my family. That didn't work out well for him because I still did what I wanted to do. The arguments became unbearable at times, but there were some occasions when he picked arguments with me so that he had a reason to spend time with other people (women, in particular). My family didn't like him at all because he was using me and not doing right by my children. My mom actually called him a "sorry excuse for a man."

Even to this day, he's still trying to control things through my daughter—and we're not even together anymore! Sometimes in my home, the things I say don't even matter to my daughter because he has told her something completely different. Unfortunately, he has come between the relationship with my daughter and me. It's nothing like it should be. I'm trying to get it re-established, but it's difficult because she won't budge. He has my daughter believing everything we went through during our relationship was all my fault and that he had no part because *(as he says)* I was the instigator of every argument. He also told her that I treat her a certain way because of how my own mother treated me, which is another one of his **lies**. He's now trying to turn my son against me with my daughter's help by her telling him he doesn't have to listen to what I say. My daughter actually tells him she doesn't care what I said he needs to do! Regardless of how she feels, I am the parent and should be respected. Sometimes, I feel like I can't win for losing with her. I know I have been called every name in the book beside my own government name when it comes to me being mentioned by that man, but not necessarily to my daughter because he knows she just might come back and tell me. *She hasn't even given my husband a chance to get to know her, all because of what her dad told her.*

I honestly never thought this man would pull out a weapon on me over a simple argument. The verbal and physical abuse were just as much of a shock from the beginning to the end. I even had a fan thrown at me over an argument about my 16-year-old cousin living with us because he felt guilty about trying to mess her. My cousin then left my house and ended up getting pregnant with her 3rd child. For a while, I had the baby on the weekends and soon after, let the baby move in with us. In my head and heart, I really wanted the baby to stay, but I also had a gut feeling that I should send her back to her mom because I felt like he was going to do something to the baby. I sent the baby back, and I guess my cousin felt like something wasn't right because when she examined her baby, she found marks that looked like someone had been pinching her. Of course, he denied everything else, so why **wouldn't** he deny doing that, too? When the baby was old enough to talk, she confirmed what I already knew: He was pinching and hitting her for nothing. She also went on to say that as long as he was around, she didn't want to be left alone with him. *I don't understand how a person could do something so evil to an innocent child just because of the dislike you have for the mother…*

From the start, I knew my children were going to be treated like outsiders. My children were always treated differently by his family as if they weren't even relatives. Who gives children hand-me-down clothes for Christmas? His mom. That's who! All of them thought it was cool and the only thing he had to say about it was, *"Well, they didn't know they were going to be here. It's the thought that counts."* One Christmas, they went to the dollar store to buy my daughter a stuffed teddy bear and my son a few cars to play with, as if I wasn't going to notice where they came from. That's so sad. It's even sadder when your child asks, *"Who are these people?"*, because she doesn't know any of them from Adam and Eve. It was as if his family knew something I needed to know and refused to say anything about whatever it was. My children and I felt isolated from the world, especially when around his family. In reverse, my children knew **my** family **very well** because they were around them often and had formed a special bond.

When money was spent, this same man would tell my kids, *"If anybody asks who bought your shoes, clothes, or anything, tell them I did or that your mother and I went half on everything."* What a bald-faced lie! He hardly did **anything** for our family. Not that it mattered, though. I always made a way to provide for my children, whether or not he helped.

I knew marrying him would have been the biggest mistake of my life. I turned down his 2nd proposal with the quickness! I also turned him down for the sake of my children as well because they **definitely** didn't like him for who he was and the things he did to me. He believed that twisting my wrist or talking to me any kind of way wasn't abuse because he did those things to "get me back in line." When he barked orders, he expected me to jump at the sound of his voice. If I didn't move when he said "MOVE!", that brought on an argument. A lot of times, my older boys weren't around to witness the arguing and bickering when they happened.

One time, I got a car from my stepdad. It didn't have any heat or air conditioning. That didn't stop him from having me pack up my kids in the cold to take him back and forth to work. That right there truly let me know he only cared about himself and not the safety of the children and me.

This man lied so much, he once told this lady he was dating that he needed to get my children some things for school and that he wanted her to give the money to him so that he could say he bought it. This same lady called me asking questions to find out the truth **and** to inform me that if I planned on picking him up from work on this particular day, he intended on killing me in front of my son. After that call, she moved on with her life without him, but I did thank her for getting in touch with me to let me know the danger I was in.

Funny thing: His mom and stepdad told him they didn't like the way I talked to him. **What about the way he spoke crazy to and abused me?** There was nothing to be said about him putting his hands on me and verbally abusing me in front of my children every day. Sadly, my older boys have picked up those same traits. I keep trying to explain to them they will get in a world of trouble if they don't stop—**NOW!** It's not at all okay for a man **OR** woman to be abusive in any way. The victims of abuse are often left with lifelong, invisible scars.

Throughout those 14 years, I tried to end the relationship with my "baby's daddy" countless times, but he threatened not only me; he also threatened to do something to my family. He **also** threatened to do something to my sister's vehicle because he knew she couldn't stand him because of all the drama he caused.

In June 2014, he put his hands on me for the last time by choking me as I was on my way to pick up my daughter from school. My husband *(who was my boyfriend at the time)* came to the scene, but my "baby's daddy" wouldn't get out of the car. I suppose he was too scared to fight a **MAN**.

Today, my husband is the best thing that ever happened to me. He saved my life by removing me from that horrible situation once and for all. I hate that I ended up involving him in the situation, but I thank God every day for him and the changes we have both made over the years.

Discussion Questions

1. What are some ways you can easily identify that a child is being abused, especially when the child is unable to vocalize the pain?

___

2. If you have a strained relationship with anyone in your family or your significant other, how can you begin to repair those relationships?

_____
_____
_____
_____
_____
_____
_____
_____
_____
_____
_____
_____
_____
_____
_____
_____
_____
_____
_____

Tosha R. Dearbone

Shade: No More Pain

Delanishia Woods

"The will of God will never take you where the grace of God will not protect you."
~ Author Unknown ~

HISTORY REPEATED: BROKEN BY HOPE

I remember being a little girl, watching my mom get abused physically, mentally, and verbally by the men she was with. As a child, it was sad and scary to see. Over and over again, I would see her cry, pick up her feelings, and keep it pushing as if nothing ever happened. I wanted so badly to help her, but I couldn't. I didn't know how. When I became a teenager, I was then old enough to know the abuse wasn't right: *"Love"* shouldn't hurt like that.

I never really understood how someone could endure a repeated cycle of hurt and pain and not make a move. Why not choose to do something different—not just for themselves, but also for the children given to them by God? I would often tell myself, *"When I get married and have kids, I'll* **NEVER** *let that happen to me. My children will* **NEVER** *see me get abused."* Little did I know the enemy already had plans to break my spirit **EARLY** in life to start the cycle of my lack of self-esteem and not knowing my true worth.

You see, I didn't have a spiritual foundation while growing up. I used to beg my mother to let me go to church, but she always said *"No."* I knew of God, but I didn't know **WHO HE TRULY WAS** (there was always a longing of "wanting to know" inside of me that I couldn't explain). At the age of 16, I, too, began my journey of becoming a victim of abuse. The cycle of abuse continued in my life for 13 years, but I'll only discuss the first five here.

I was working my first job at Popeye's when "he" walked in with his friends. *"Welcome to Popeye's. How many I help you?"* I asked. *"By letting me get your number,"* came the response. He was a little older than I, and the fact that he was interested in me (of *ALL* people) had my heart racing. I gave him my number. It didn't take long **AT ALL** for me to fall "in love." He said all the right things, had graduated from high school, and he had a job and car (I later found out the car belonged to his mother). This man opened an invitation to a life that was more *appealing* than the one I was living at home, where I was helping my grandmother raise my brothers and sisters.

In a matter of just a few weeks, I was a completely different person. Some of my decisions caused me to be put out of my mother's house because I was "too grown" and felt I could "handle life on my own." After all, I did have a boyfriend who had his own car and apartment. I didn't need "home" anymore, right?

It didn't take long for a sexually-transmitted disease (STD) to enter my new realm of life. Thank God, it was curable because my life would look much different today if it weren't. I was angry, hurt, confused, and knew nothing more to do but stay. Staying is what I had seen while growing up. I then found out he was still having sex with the mother of his first child.

He loved ME, he said.

He didn't mean for it to happen, he said.

It will never happen again, he said.

I remember going to her house with him a lot of times. I would sit in the car in the driveway and wait for him to finish "visiting his child." One day, his friend went with us. He and I were in the car for a very long time, so he went in to check on what was taking so long. He returned to the car **angry**. I asked him, *"What's wrong?"*

"You are too sweet of a girl," he said. *"You should leave him."*

I wasn't stupid. I put two and two together, but he loved **ME**...didn't he? I mean, that's what he said. For whatever the reason, that's what I believed. This was love—the way I learned it to be. It didn't come easy. You just played the cards you were dealt.

I was still going to school every day, and then...the morning sickness started. Pregnant at the age of 16. My mother and I didn't have the best relationship, but it still scared the life out of me. I called and told her I was pregnant. It broke my heart to break the news to my grandmother, though. My mother wanted me to have an abortion. That infuriated me because she had **ME** at 16 years old! I had learned enough in health class to know abortion was something I didn't believe in. So, I kept my child.

Due to my pregnancy, I had to switch schools. I enrolled in a school that would allow me to complete my work at a faster pace in hopes of graduating sooner. They had strict rules, such as I could not miss one day. If I needed to be late because of a doctor's appointment, my mother would have to let them know. Being that I wasn't living at home, I had to let my mother know when I had an appointment so that when the school called, she could verify my whereabouts. One morning, my mother's spite reared its ugly head. I arrived at school one afternoon with a doctor's note in hand and was told I could no longer attend classes there. They had called my mom, and she claimed to have no knowledge of me having a doctor's appointment. I was mad and heartbroken. **Why did she do that to me?**

So now, I was 16, pregnant, living with a boyfriend who was cheating on me, and unable to further my education. Being with him full time allowed me to see the things he was doing when I wasn't around. I then spoke up for myself: *"You are **NOT** going to keep doing me like this! I am having your child!"* The abuse started subtly with him pushing me up against walls or down on the couch, telling me to get out of his way and that he was a grown man who would do what he wanted to do. In response, I would push him back. He put his hand around my throat and squeezed...hard. I would hit him back to defend myself. He'd leave. I'd cry, pick up my feelings, and continue like nothing was wrong. He would always come back and apologize for his earlier actions—and promised to never treat me like that again.

When I was 17 ½ years old, my daughter was born. That didn't make things better. The arguing and fighting got worse, and the make-up sex sessions would happen. Within a couple of months of having my first child, I was pregnant with my second. My life was not going according to the dreams I had once envisioned. He wouldn't get a job, and the only thing I knew to do was work. I did, after all, have 1 ½ children to care for and a roof to keep over our heads. If there was one thing I learned from my mother, it was a good work ethic. I worked two, sometimes three jobs, while he sat and reaped the benefits.

His frustration with not having enough money caused him to turn to a life of crime. He would rob drunk people at night as they walked down the street, kick in doors to homes, and boost goods from department stores (which is where I was used). He had a friend who worked security at a two-story department store. On days they had pre-arranged, his friend would unplug the alarm sensor so that when someone would walk past with stolen goods, it wouldn't go off. I was to get on the elevator and meet his friend upstairs, where he had preselected expensive clothes and jackets. I would then get back on the elevator with him and the items as if I was going to pay for the merchandise downstairs. As soon as the doors would close, he would pull out two huge store bags that were folded small in his uniform. We had to get all of the items into the bags before the elevator made it to the first floor and the doors opened. I then casually walked out and headed straight to the car. Was I scared out of my mind? Yes, I was! The thought that I could go to jail crossed my mind.

Let me tell you how the hand of God will cover you, even in the stupidest of life's moments. The enemy only has so much power when, at the end of it all, there is a promise on your life. When I realized I could go to jail and have my unborn baby while there, and that my daughter would be without her mother, I said, *"NO MORE!"*

I am unsure what "clicked" for him, but one day, he came home and announced he was entering the military. Looking back on this now, I see it was my moment to get away…but I didn't. What had me so stuck? Well, he said he was going to make me his wife and do right by his family. I believed that marrying him would make everything better. Maybe it would make him treat me better, especially since our second child was on the way. This **HAD** to be a good decision, right?

I was a little over 18 years old when he graduated from boot camp. His mother, my baby girl, and I flew to Great Lakes, Illinois to see him graduate. He wanted to marry me **THAT** weekend. He wasn't able to spend much time with us to help "plan the wedding," so I dug into the Yellow Pages (for the millennials, that's a paper phone book; I couldn't just "Ask Google") and called around. In that small military town, a lot of things were closed because it was the weekend. I finally reach a pastor. I explained our situation, and he welcomed us to come to his home.

We arrived the following day. The pastor asked us some questions, including if we were *sure* getting married is what we wanted to do. We both said *"Yes!"*, and with the pastor's wife, my soon-to-be mother-in-law, and our daughter standing there as witnesses, we were married. I got married in the living room of a stranger's home in jeans and a sweater. It was *not* the fairytale wedding most young girls picture themselves having…

So, there I was: 18, married to someone who cheated on me, gave me an STD, abused me physically, and beat me down mentally. I would never participate in a high school graduation, senior prom, class trip, or gain lifelong friends with whom I could go to college. Nope. None of that. I was a wife now, and I was hopeful that one day, things would all work out.

I returned home, and shortly after gave birth to my son. I packed up and moved to a small military town in Georgia — **many** miles away from everything and everyone I knew. But this was good, right? Remember: I'm married now, so the lying, cheating, and abuse would stop, right? **WRONG!** *It only got worse!*

I spiraled into someone I didn't even recognize (not that I knew who I was, to begin with). To keep "my man" happy, I did things I wasn't raised to do just to show faithfulness and loyalty to a man who didn't demonstrate the same. I began drinking and smoking cigarettes to fit in. I engaged in sex acts that defiled my marriage bed because he had fantasies he wanted to fulfill and, as his wife, I needed to uphold my "wifely duties" of honoring him. I was so lost…so numb. I remember going into the bathroom one night and sitting up against the bathroom door. I ran water in the tub so he couldn't hear me cry. I then pulled out the knife I had with me and pressed it into my wrist. I didn't want to kill myself; I just wanted the pain of my life to stop. I knew that if I pressed hard enough, the pain would cease—at least for a second. But I digressed. I had children who needed **ME**.

Arguments always turned physical, and as much as I didn't want to expose my children to the violence, he didn't care. Even though they were toddlers, I knew it was something they shouldn't see. Leaving him was not an option because those were "his kids," he said. He threatened me by saying things like, *"I'm a military man now. They will be on my side. You wouldn't get the kids if you left."*

One night while we were fighting, he bit me on the back of my arm as hard as he could. The next morning, I had a softball-sized black and purple bruise that took forever to heal. Soon after that fight, I went home to visit my grandmother. Texas summers are hot, and you can only put on so many clothes before you begin to sweat your life away. As such, it didn't take long for her to see my arm. *"What happened to you, Tanka?"* (Tanka is the nickname she gave me.)

Shade: No More Pain

"Nothing, Mama. I was playing around and fell into something. It's okay. I'm fine," I replied.

My grandmother was no fool. She knew exactly what happened. *"You know, Tanka, if you need to, you can always come back home and stay with Mama. You know that, don't you?"*

"Yes, ma'am." Thank God for planted seeds.

I returned to Georgia and time passed. Lots of time. He was gone on deployments, and time did **NOT** make my heart grow fonder. He would come back still "him."

One day, I came home from work, and there was a car in the driveway. As I approached the front door, something said, *"Turn the knob quietly."* I listened to that voice. The living room was empty. As I walked deeper into the house, I could hear the kids playing in their room in the back of the house. Where was he? I made my way down the hall towards our bedroom. The door was closed. When I opened it, there they were; he and a woman he worked with. They were in **OUR** bed while **OUR** kids were in the next room! I recall my world going dark at that moment. I didn't even make a scene. I just left.

I couldn't breathe. I couldn't form a thought.

I got into the car and drove to a nearby park on base and just cried. My soul was crushed. I cried out, **"God, help me...please?"** I didn't know my Heavenly Father well at that point. I didn't even know if He heard me. What I **DID** know was that I needed something to happen.

I went back home, silent. I had no words. I had become numb to the "I'm sorrys" over time. His words had stopped having meaning some time ago. I knew he would be going on another deployment soon and decided that was when I would do it; I would leave him. That's just what I did. I packed nothing more than clothes for my children and me. I wanted nothing else from that life. Meanwhile, my grandmother's words played over and over again in my mind:

"You can always come stay with Mama. You know that, right?"

The kids and I got into the minivan, headed down I-10, and never looked back. It was no one but God who gave me the courage to make that move. With my broken spirit and the lack of belief and confidence I had in myself, I know I would have never done it on my own.

I let my children's father know I wanted a divorce. He tried his hardest to get me to come back and threatened to take the kids if I didn't return. ***"Go ahead and TRY it,"*** I said with boldness. **ONLY GOD** knows where that newfound strength and confidence came from! Soon after that conversation, I turned 21.

From a child of 16 to a woman (by age only) of 21, I had endured a lifetime of lessons in a matter of just a few years.

I share this story in hopes of it reaching the heart and mind of a young lady who may find herself in a similar situation today. Walk away. **RUN** away if you have to. There are people who care and who will listen to the cry of your soul **IF** you just tell someone. I could have easily lost my life several times and not be here today to share this with you. But **GOD** kept me — and **HE** has kept you, too. You're here for a reason, and it's *NOT* to be hurt by someone who is broken themselves. You have a purpose. You are a light which is to be shared with the world (read Matthew 5:14-16), not one to be shut up in darkness because of your pains and bruises.

You are **GOD'S DAUGHTER!** Own it because **THAT'S** what's **REAL!**

Discussion Questions

1. How can raising children in an abusive environment affect them as they get older?

2. What are some actions you would take to prevent yourself from contracting an STD?

_____
_____
_____
_____
_____
_____
_____
_____
_____
_____
_____
_____
_____
_____
_____
_____
_____
_____
_____
_____
_____
_____

3. If you were in an abusive relationship, would you reach out for help (even if it's not to family) **OR** would you keep what you're going through to yourself? Explain your choice.

___
___
___
___
___
___
___
___
___
___
___
___
___
___
___
___
___
___
___
___
___

Shade: No More Pain

LaTonya L. Jones

"Never bend your head. Always hold it high. Look the world straight in the face."
~ Helen Keller ~

Tosha R. Dearbone

NO PAIN, NO GAIN

When you see the title of my story, I imagine the legendary Betty Wright's song, "No Pain, No Gain," popped into your head. In her song, she paints this picture that you must go through something to gain something.

What happens when you have done all you can do, and you still end up with an abusive man?

It seems like from an early age, I had a target on my back to be abused in one way or another. I never asked for the little boy to place his hands down my pants. Neither did I welcome the threat to have a guy come to my school and burn my hair off because I wasn't allowed to date. Then, there was the guy who was way older than me who couldn't seem to keep his hands to himself. I was so afraid to tell my dad that this dude was touching me inappropriately because I was "proud" that he was going to church. I didn't want to take that away from him. Although I was taught that abuse was **not** okay, I seemed to leap into a marriage in which I thought my demise would come one of two ways; either I was going to kill myself or he was going to kill me.

One of my fears was that he was going to kill me because his anger was so bad. No matter how much I tried to please him, it was never enough. I had no idea I was married to a narcissist. When we first got married, he did everything in his power to keep me happy and do all the things that I loved. That soon changed. If you have never been married to someone who had terrible habits such as drug and alcohol use, let me tell you this: The fight can be more significant than you could ever know. The more my husband consumed alcohol and abused drugs, I had a glimpse of a different man — one I didn't know.

There were a couple of moments in the marriage that made me change my perception of love. They made me think there may have been something wrong with me. I must share my story because there may be a woman out there married who was told the same lies that I've been told.

I know that in marriage, sex is one of the major elements. However, **NO** still means **NO**. Whoever created that whole tale about, *"He is your husband. It's not rape,"* is a pure **IDIOT!** If he is screaming, physically abusing you, and telling you he will get it from someone else just to get you to have sex when you're unwilling, he is attempting to manipulate you so that he can get his way.

I remember the following night as if it were yesterday...

My now-ex-husband wanted to have sex, and I told him *"NO!"* I knew to deny him his want was a bad idea, simply because he was drinking at the time. When he drank and did his "poison of choice," he was a different character. That night, I must have been asking for trouble because I tried to stand my ground and tell him that I wasn't laying down with him — at least not in the condition he was in. I feel that he ignored my *"NO!"* Immediately, he ripped off my clothes. My mind raced because he was someone I trusted and loved, yet there he was violating me...and there was nothing I could do about it. The more I kicked, screamed, and tried to run away, the angrier he grew. I finally tired of running and crying and asked him not to do what he intended because it would change the element of our relationship. I was apparently talking to a wall because my panties were then ripped off of me, followed by his fingers harshly jammed inside of me. Soon after, his man part penetrated my sacred spot. The more I cried, the more fuel it gave to him to get his release. Once he reached his peak, he walked away as if nothing happened.

The next day, my body was sore and bruised from trying to get away from him and his grabbing of my arms and legs during the rape. *(If it walks and quacks like a duck, it's a duck. Let's call it what it is.)* The rape left me with hard questions that needed answers.

- **How do you recover from someone holding you down, forcing himself inside of you?**
- **How do you recover from him choking you because he didn't agree with something you said?**
- **How do you hide bruises and depression from people you trust?**

Unfortunately, I hid a lot of things deep inside for a long time while trying to protect him. It wasn't all love; most was for my children's sake. I was experiencing toxic love at its finest, yet at the moment, I had no clue what that was. What I did know was that all I was going through was my fault. I was to blame for all the things I experienced with him. Had I known then that I was not in a healthy relationship and none of it was my fault, I would have walked away a lot sooner.

There were moments that led up to me knowing I was in an abusive relationship, but I ignored every signal given for the greater good of my family. My mental and physical wellbeing were never as important to me then as they are now. I should have had this mindset all along, as I didn't deserve to be abused and that my *"NO!"* meant **"NO!"** Because he was so close to me, it was easy for him to manipulate my mind by making me feel both guilty and like I was always in the wrong.

Many days, I considered committing suicide. Other days, I actually acted on those thoughts because I felt that was my only way out. I had no family support because he had my entire family wrapped around his finger. I couldn't even trust what the pastor of the church I was attending at the time said because both my then-husband and the pastor were "old school" and tried to set the picture that things between us weren't that bad. The pastor said I needed to stay with my husband and stick by his side.

For a long time, I suffered in silence…alone. I was too embarrassed to tell anyone that I was being abused. Every chance he had, he tried to cut me with his words. Verbal abuse is just as toxic. For a little while, that form of abuse worked. One day, however, a switch on the inside of me went off when my thoughts were filled with finding ways to kill him. When I arrived at **THAT** place, I knew it was time for me to go and let him go his way. The fact that he had taunted me mentally, physically, verbally, and emotionally left me with no choice but to harm him as much (if not more than) he hurt me.

Fortunately for him, it's not in my nature to harm anyone.

This is what you should know: What saved his life is that I have a praying mother **AND** my relationship with God means more to me than sitting in jail. I prayed and told God, *"You* **MUST** *remove him, or I'm going to kill him!"* I could no longer tolerate him or his behavior.

I woke up one day and decided to put me first. I couldn't care about what the church or my family said. Until this day, a lot of them have stories and an image of me that is untrue and inaccurate. This, however, is the year the truth will be exposed! I chose to no longer hang onto something that was dead and had no plans on growing. Do you know what it feels like to be with someone who refuses to grow? Perhaps you already know what it feels like to carry them and you. Can you say "EXHAUSTING"?

For me, I had to mentally get to a place where I wanted to live. I knew I was more than what he said and how he made me feel. That's when LaTonya got up and took her life back! I didn't have to leave him because he left me. He was, of course, upset that I finally decided to call it quits. Not only did he leave me; he took my children with him as punishment to me. As you can see, the abuse didn't stop—even though we were separated. I had to learn to set boundaries when it came to him.

At some point, I found **"ME."** I knew I had to push my way past the pains of sexual, physical, and emotional abuse. At the time I was going through this transformation, I must admit that I **never** thought about openly sharing my story for other women and young ladies to read. I was never open to sharing my story publicly because I was too ashamed. I am not excited that I went through the things I did, but I am *thrilled* to share my story and tell you how I overcame those trials and tribulations.

So, you want to know how I snapped back, huh? I'm glad that you asked!

I relocated out of the same city as him. I continued my education and graduated with my Master's Degree in Education. I bought my first car all by myself with **no** help. I moved into my own place. I began to work on my health for the better. After battling high blood pressure, I lost some weight after being over 200 pounds. I started to put myself and my needs first. I started recognizing that I was "the s**t," regardless if anyone else told me or not. I also worked on rebuilding my relationship with the Lord by praying, meditating, and studying His Word. That is where my real 'glow-up' came from.

Remember, Sis:
There is nothing sexier than a woman who is of a straight mind, body, and soul.

When you decide to take your life and power back, you have already won the battle. Never be ashamed to get counseling to discuss what you are dealing with. Acknowledging that I needed to talk to someone was one of the hardest things I've ever had to do. I always believed therapy was for people with **DEEP** issues. It took me some time to realize I had **DEEP** issues that I tried to cover up. Little did I know: Covering up my **DEEP** issues was causing difficulties in how I mothered my children, had relationships with other people, and how I viewed myself.

Never let someone make you feel you must brush being abused under the rug! No! Get help and heal from it so that you can help another woman push through.

Loving me and restoring myself was the **BEST** thing I could have ever done for myself.

Healing was the **BEST** thing I could have ever done for myself.

Sharing this with you is the **BEST** thing I could have ever done for **US**.

No longer will I hide in the dark because of the things that have been done to me. I have been quiet for far too long — silent because I never wanted to be viewed as a "weirdo." These are feelings many women live with daily. They hide and stay silent, suffering in silence.

Today, **WOMAN**, I encourage you to step out of the darkness and into the light. Heal! No one ever said the process would be easy but know that you are not alone. I, for one, am praying and rooting for you and your wholeness. Wake up each morning and tell yourself that you are great and are *NOT* your past. The person who violated you in any way does not have power over you.

That was how I overcame those ugly wounds that I kept covered for so long. Had I never had someone who had been through what I have gone through to push me and tell me I **CAN** heal and love again, I would still be bitter and angry.

****

Sis,

    Don't apologize for wanting to heal and love again. That healing may come from confronting your abuser or perhaps spending a day locked away in your room writing a letter to your broken self. If you opt for the latter, burn it and keep it moving. Do not be afraid to love and embrace what comes naturally. Love does not hurt. Forget what you heard. Do not feel guilty because you need to spend a little extra time on you. Please do, Sis! If we all took the time to heal and work on us, we would be so much better and not out here hurting each other. Pray, meditate, and stay in your Word. Doing so will remind you that you are **MORE** than a conqueror. Know that you have sisters near and far awaiting your "come up." Take those scars and make them beautiful. Write a book, work on a movie script, create a women's group, speak at the women's shelter—do whatever it takes! Don't you dare give up!

    I love you and await your **GLOW-UP**!

Love Yours Truly,

LaTonya

Discussion Questions

1. What will you do to work towards your healing today?

_____
_____
_____
_____
_____
_____
_____
_____
_____
_____
_____
_____
_____
_____
_____
_____

2. Have you set boundaries with people during your healing process? If so, what are they? If not, what's preventing you from doing so?

_____
_____
_____
_____
_____
_____
_____
_____
_____
_____
_____
_____
_____
_____
_____
_____
_____
_____
_____

3. Will you commit to speaking positive things into your life daily? Write at least five (5) "I AM" affirmations you will commit to memory.

_____
_____
_____
_____
_____
_____
_____
_____
_____
_____
_____
_____
_____
_____
_____
_____
_____

Shade: No More Pain

Joslyn Curley

"How you love yourself is how you teach others to love you."
~ **Rupi Kaur** ~

UNCHAINED

Up until now, I just **knew** I could handle anything that came my way. I finished college, started a business, and managed to spend an astonishing **3,000 hours** absorbed in mental health counseling. Of course, there were times when I wasn't always secure in how I managed life, but I tried hard to achieve those things I felt were necessary. I worked hard and set reasonable goals. I set out to do the unexpected—sometimes too much. I want what everyone else thinks they want: My own sense of happiness. While on my journey through life, I spent time and money on efforts that ultimately did not bring me joy. And that, my friends, is the challenging part of life.

God supplies our needs; not our wants.

It's incredible the things I have done and accomplished versus what brings me down. I work hard to hide that side of me, as if I'm invincible.

The truth is I am a grown kid who sometimes allows words to hurt me—**OR** is it from whom those words flow that sets me off these days? *Hmm…*

Well, 2019 is a brand-new year. No longer will I allow any more bulls**t. I finally decided that after years of battling with therapist after therapist (ones who only tried to assist me in gaining control of my life), I was no longer going to tolerate any more crap. Over the last 20 years, I have seen a "few" therapists; however, the most recent one is **soooo** different. I found her on an African-American website along with a list of her specializations. I knew I needed someone tough, yet fair;

empathetic, yet unapologetic; and, furthermore, not a friend or colleague of mine. I needed a downright truth-teller who didn't care how I felt.

First, I prayed. Then, I prayed some more. Was this lady going to lead me to some truths I could deal with, help me move on to being truly happy, and stop me from pretending? Would she guide me to strength, understanding, and vital coping skills? Would I need my own transformation? Stepping out on faith, I called and set an appointment.

I met her about a week later. The first impression was that she seemed friendly and pleasant. From the onset, we made an unusual agreement: I would let her know immediately of any concerns about her services, and I requested that she not be my friend (in this business, friends don't mix well). Although we are both clinicians, it was imperative that we both remain professional. I wanted her to be truthful, honest, and fair with me.

That first meeting was almost seven months ago (at the time of this writing). Ever since, I have seen her weekly for about six months and recently went to every two weeks. Each session with her, I cried. She brought up things so deep in my childhood that they would resonate an incident or event that had a hold of me. Each time while in session, something traumatic would trigger a sense of isolation or neglect within me.

Wait. What? I was **neglected** as a child? I understood the *isolation* (I'll explain that later), but *neglect*???

Our sessions were like mini-lectures on how my family dynamic was unique. I mean, I knew that everybody had some form of dysfunction in their family. Mine was no different, right? **WRONG!** My therapist would state the obvious, and I would change her words to suit my disbelief. I never wanted to acknowledge the dysfunction in my family. It was simpler to assume I — alone — was the problem. This is where the isolation comes in. You see, instead of my family owning their individual issues, it was easier for them to put their issues on me and make me accountable, leaving me feeling unloved and unsupported.

Even as I continue therapy today, that casting of their issues continues to happen.

When my therapist informed me of the neglect, I did not want to believe her. I was defensive and told her she was wrong. She, in turn, told me why she felt that way. I mean, sure I spent time alone, had no friends, was surrounded by **no** other children the same age as I in my neighborhoods, did not spend time with cousins, etc. I could see why she would say that.

There was no childhood in my childhood.

Both of my parents worked full-time jobs. They did not help with schoolwork. There were no extra-curricular activities — no matter how much I persisted. Living on the North side of Houston, it seemed as if we lived far away from what others might consider normalcy. I also noticed my family rarely participated in activities or, for that matter, communicated with each other. We kind of went about our lives and rarely spoke to each other, unless there was something corrective being stated or a chore assigned.

I began to look at my life as an individual. My typical school day consisted of going to school, coming home, finishing my work *(sometimes)*, and watching videos. There was no one to talk to, no one to whom I could relate, and no one to call a "friend." I would *isolate* myself in my room...until disagreements started. Periodically, there would be yelling, cursing, and violence. My sister closed her door; mine was always open. Due to the chaos, coupled with all the time I spent alone, my longing to be happy was monumental. Even still, through all the dysfunction, I sincerely loved my family. Our lifestyle was all I knew. *Until recently, I thought that was normal...*

All of my life, I was told I was just like my father. He's kind, hilarious, and loving. I was told I *looked* like my mother; pretty. She's also loving and encouraging. However, everyone has a difficult side. My dad could be a beast when he wanted; my mom could be rude and unfair. As they have aged, those facets of their personalities continue to show even more. Although I had the privilege to mend with my father when he was baptized some years ago and decided to work on better relationships with his children, I haven't completely forgotten everything that momentarily separated us. As for my mother and I, we have an entirely different relationship altogether.

After discovering (*or **rediscovering***) my childhood, I was able to put some things into perspective. However, one thing I could never clearly understand was why all the negativity seemed to flow back to my mother. Now, don't get me wrong: My father wasn't perfect, but the imperfections of my mother seemed to hold me back and basically hurt me later in life. The biggest misconception is my mother's ability to catch me at vulnerable times and advocate for me. For instance, when I was sick, she liked to attend the appointments so that she could be sure the doctor gets the "whole story," yet it was never the **complete** story. The doctors would get a version of me being unable to take care of myself, when I would have **never** spoken that to them directly and given them my input. Even now, I am way over the age of eighteen, and each doctor has yet to hear my side of the story. I can't fail to mention the doctors my mom usually supported always adored her and didn't like to answer my questions. There were also many ruined relationships and friendships based on her speculations or experiences that she had.

Honestly, if I could rewind the tape, I'm pretty sure my mother gave up on me when I got into a fight in high school. I believe that to be true because I recall moving further away from a relationship with her and building a closer one with my father. She always seemed to try to slow me down—and I was never purposely fast! Let me explain:

For example, I would do things on purpose just to get on her nerves. That would include something like meeting up with people she disliked. My actions were often in response to something she said or did to me. I'll never understand the unusual relationship I had with her. It's like a secret nobody wanted to let me in on. Nothing I did ever pleased her, so I accepted my role in the family. I filled in the blanks. Eventually, I simply became numb to how I really felt and settled for playing the "backseat" for several years. I would stop and have moments of clarity, trying to defend myself. Sadly, it seemed as if I was the **ONLY** one fighting for *ME*...for my *sanity*...for *normalcy*.

To this day, the problem remains that I love my family. I despise what we've become **without** the support of family therapy, but it seems to be too late now. Everyone is set in their ways and "ready to retire." All I have left is to think solely about myself. I cannot worry about whether or not someone else is getting it, wanting to understand, or in need of having their own questions answered.

I have exhausted all close friendships with my story. I have attempted to pay back everyone in my family for their random acts of kindness. I have made my last attempt at Sunday dinners that end with me feeling unwelcomed or unwanted before I start **MY** week.

*I was **DONE** with trying.*

Ever since I was young, I would hide the chaos with my silent agenda. I would load myself up with so many things to do that I was not paying attention to what was happening around me—a skill I learned from my mother. For example, she would never pass up an opportunity to get me the books I wanted from the Book Club. I always had the latest New Edition cassette tape to listen to. With my mom's credit cards, I always had the latest gear to keep up with the other kids in my neighborhood (ones I was never friends with anyway).

Regarding the neglect my therapist initially told me about, you could add self-isolation to that list. I was used to coming home, being alone with my books and music…and in my own thoughts. As I grew older, I performed the same way. I would load myself up with academics, goals, silent achievements, etc., to keep me busy. Every job or position I went after, I would get. My majors, jobs, electives, master's, sorority, and most recently a doctorate would grow progressively harder. I tried being social, but I just never quite fit in. I did what I had to do to take my mind off of my silent cries—until I met my current therapist.

My therapist has consistently remained center stage. When others gently slid off the merry-go-round, she prevailed. I appreciate her quiet, caring consistency. She only offers words of praise and encourages ownership of my abilities and acceptance of my past. She has spurred me to ask my own questions to those so-called doctors who seem to know my whole life with one incident. She stops me when I press too hard in my dialogue with her, and it touches her heart—reflecting that it profoundly affects me. She tells me I have worked hard and am of value. And she makes me run…**so fast** that I feel all of me and my breath leaving my body. I thank God for her in my life. She has taught me something I haven't known in a while: Next to God, Joslyn comes first.

*To you I say: Get yourself a **GOOD** therapist!*

Now, I have made a decision. I have decided to trust in God. I don't want to know about others' relationships with God; I am on a quest to find my own journey. I'm good, but I want to be **GREAT** with Him. I am determined to "fill my cup until it runneth over" with Christians because I have decided that all I do and will do is for God and His people. I have decided to dream. I have decided to make my plans. I have decided to execute those plans. I have decided to surround myself with like-minded people who do the same. I didn't even know those types of people were out there! Trust me; they are.

What I have learned is that you have to do a little research about yourself. After all, if you love yourself, why not? Take that chance and invest in a little something called **YOU**. Make **YOU** the best brand possible. Take the leap of faith and do those things that make you happy—no matter how unconventional.

*The world can be whatever you make it;
just make it a happy place.*

My bottom line is this: I tend to be conservative in concluding that words **DO** hurt. Although a person may not physically attack and make you feel low, the intensity of someone's **WORDS** can penetrate and attempt to destroy you. Even though I was never truly physically abused (never beyond corrective spankings), I was emotionally abused. Abuse of any kind is disheartening, especially when you cannot retaliate because you believe what the scriptures say: *"Honor thy mother and thy father."* As a child, there aren't many options for retaliation. However, dealing with it now, I know I **DO** have choices.

So, what do you do when approached in a negative way in which you cannot openly disagree? Distance yourself and love from that distance.

What hurts me to the core is that people rarely change. As time goes on, they get set in their ways, stop caring, and don't change for the better. It's sad that I cannot erase time and start over with the knowledge about people that I have now. I can only hope that for everyone I hope to see again in the next lifetime, they will see a **GOOD** therapist in Heaven and that they love God and all of His children.

Discussion Questions

1. What do you believe was the **biggest** issue with the author's mother?

_____
_____
_____
_____
_____
_____
_____
_____
_____
_____
_____
_____
_____
_____
_____
_____

2. Would you say her father and sister were contributors to her family's dysfunctional dynamic? If so, how?

3. In what ways do you feel it's possible for parents to be enablers for their children well into adulthood?

Tragula Speaks

"The Gospel offers forgiveness for the past, new life for the present, and hope for the future."
~ John Sentamu ~

Tosha R. Dearbone

NEW LIFE IS JUST OVER THE HORIZON

I am the product of a single mother of four children from the small town of Marvell, Arkansas. When I was growing up, the population was less than 1,500 people. My graduating class consisted of an estimated 30 people. Marvell was a poverty-stricken town. Jobs were scarce and practically the entire community qualified for low-income assistance.

Mom wasn't always single, though. The only father figure I had in my life with any consistency was my little brother's father. I remember him being there for us solely as a provider. He wasn't that type of dad who played with us, took us out to do fun things, or taught us about life. I actually recall him working a lot and not really being around often.

With my mom being the sole provider for my three siblings and me, she had to work two jobs to care for us. That was difficult for her to do in a town that didn't have many jobs to begin with. Nonetheless, she worked the graveyard shift at one job and the local nursing home as a Certified Nursing Assistant (CNA) during the day. When she worked the late-night job, that meant we couldn't be left home alone because we were too young. We used to stay at either one of our two aunt's houses when mom had to work overnight.

Cousin Jimmy

Whenever I stayed at my aunt Roxanne's home, I usually slept on the couch in the living room. My cousin, Jimmy, would sometimes sleep on the opposite end. I can remember being awakened by his foot rubbing against my vagina (that happened on more than one occasion). I was around ten years old at the time. After deciding I no longer wanted to be sexually violated by Jimmy's foot, I refused to stay at aunt Roxanne's house and went to stay with my aunt, Sheila. While there, I told her what Jimmy had been doing to me. She then told my mom and aunt Roxanne. After that, I never spent another night at aunt Roxanne's house—and the incidents with Jimmy were never talked about again.

The Johnson Family

The Johnsons were a lovely family. The parents, Allen and Shelly, had two children; Shea, who was about three years older than me, and a son who was a toddler at the time. I was around 12 years old. The Johnsons worked at the school—Allen in the cafeteria and Shelly was the middle school secretary. They were trusted people in our small community. We lived across the street from the Johnsons. Shelly and my mom became good friends. In turn, Shea and I became friends. I used to go to their house and spend the night with Shea often.

Shea always wanted to play house when I visited. Most times, we did so in her bedroom with the door closed. She always kept her room dark when we played our little game. 'House' consisted of a tent in her room that was made from a sheet that was laid over pieces of bedroom furniture. While in the tent, Shea would have me do sexual things to her such as suck her breasts, rub her vagina, and kiss. We kissed a lot. This type of "play" went on for a while until it abruptly came to an end.

I never told anyone about this experience until recently because I had pushed it so far back in the recesses of my memory, I had honestly forgotten all about it.

Peep Show

My older brother, Dwayne, was a drug addict. He is six years older than me and used to steal from me, my mom, and the few stores in our small town. He stole anything he could get his hands on to supply his drug habit. Having an addict for a brother was so embarrassing.

One night, while my mom was at work and I was asleep in my bed, the sudden flash of my bedroom light coming on awakened me. Through my grogginess, I recognized my brother. He had brought someone into my room with him. As they stood over my bed, my brother lifted the covers so the boy could look at me laying there in my shirt and panties. As I came out of my deep sleep that had been disturbed, I then recognized the guy who was standing next to my brother. It was Andy. He was around the same age as me but was a school dropout. Just as fast as they entered my room and peeped under the covers at me, they were gone. I never mentioned the peep show to anyone.

It didn't take long to figure out that Dwayne had either been paid or given drugs by Andy to let him look at me partially clothed. That behavior became my brother's M.O. Some local drug boy would stop by with Dwayne when my mom wasn't home—day or night—so that whoever was with him could "see" me. He would even try to coax me into going outside to talk to the guys he would bring over. **Not only NO, but HELL NO!** Dwayne always tried to get me to date one of the local drug boys *(clearly for **HIS** benefit)*, but I wouldn't.

Never Alone

When I was 15 years old, an older boy named Rob took an interest in me. I really liked him, too. He had graduated from high school and was living at home with his parents. We had to sneak to talk to each other because there was no way my mom would approve of me talking to him.

His friend, Bernard, was already talking to and having sex with my best friend, Brittany, making it easy for Rob and I to see each other whenever the other two hooked up *(I was still a virgin at the time)*. I was also friends with Rob's cousin, Cindy. Cindy, Brittany, and I were classmates.

One day, we went over to Rob's house to hang out with the guys. His parents weren't home at the time, so he and I went into his room. I just knew that would be the day I lost my virginity, and I was ready. After all, most of my friends and other girls I hung out with had already lost their virginity. Why should I be the odd one out? Rob and I were in the room touching and kissing on one another. Suddenly, there was a loud bang on the door. It was his cousin, Donna—Cindy's sister. She said, *"I am not going to let you have sex with her!"* So, we stopped what we were doing. I immediately walked out of the room and left. Rob and I continued to see each other for a while—quick moments after games or while I was hanging out with my friends.

And the Winner Is...

My cousin, Nathan, would stay over most nights when my mom was at work *(I was in the 9th grade at this time)*. He was like the big brother I never had because my blood brother, Dwayne, was often gone for days at a time stealing, doing his drugs, or spending time in jail *(most of the time, he was in **jail**)*.

One time, I was able to sneak out of the house before Nathan came over. Rob picked me up, and we went to a dark, secluded back road. Once he parked, we hopped into the backseat of his car. In an instant, he was all over me, kissing and feeling his way all over my body. Both of us were getting sexually-aroused, so I knew what was coming next. Then, I panicked! I couldn't do it. I told him I was scared and wanted to stop. He didn't stop. He ignored my pleas. I kept saying, **"STOP! STOP! STOP!"** He then started ripping off my clothes, causing us to begin wrestling in the confines of that little space. He managed to lock both of my wrists in his hands over my head, remove my clothes, and rape me.

I stopped fighting. The cries for him to stop turned to ones of defeat. He had won the battle by overpowering me. He won by forcing himself inside of me. He won by raping me and taking away my virginity.

When he finished, we got back into the front seat and made the short trip back to my house. I got out of the car, went inside, ran myself a bath, climbed in…and cried some more. I balled myself up and rocked back and forth while my cousin, Nathan, watched television in the living room. Eventually, I got out of the tub and went to bed.

Again, I never told anyone about what happened to me.

I later learned that Rob had a girlfriend at the time he raped me. She was one grade above me. Soon after the rape, she found out about he and I. He explained me away as "the little girl who had a crush on him." His girlfriend and her friends started to taunt and make fun of me at school. I made it my business to avoid them as best I could throughout the day and at after-school activities.

Soon after that dreadful night, Rob moved away to another state. I never saw him again.

The Drug Boy Saved Me

When I was in the 10th grade, I started dating my high school sweetheart, Danny. He was a year older than me. Danny came from one of the few well-to-do families in our small town. His parents never disrespected me, but they did treat me as if I wasn't good enough for their son. His mother would do things like instruct me on how to properly chew gum and remind me of how she thought my manners should be when I sometimes traveled with them. I used to feel that she only tolerated me because I was the love of her teenage son's life. Had she actually taken the time to get to know me, she would've learned I was smart and athletic. She was an administrator at our school, and his father held a high position at one of the few places of employment near our town.

Oh, but Danny loved me, alright! He was very possessive. He wanted me to be with him all the time. We had sex all the time and talked on the phone…**ALL** the other times. When my mom worked the graveyard shift, Danny would sneak over and stay the night with me. On the nights when he didn't do that, he made sure he stayed on the phone with me until we both fell asleep. Most nights, we wouldn't hang up until it was time for my mom to come home.

I now know that was his way of keeping tabs on me, making sure I wasn't with any other guys or talking to any on the phone.

We would argue all the time about me hanging out with my friends after school, after games, and on the weekends. He expressly stated he didn't want me talking to or hanging out with **ANY** other boys. In our small town, there wasn't much to do. We would often get dressed up, just to walk around town. We hung out on the corners of the main streets where all the teens would gather to talk and listen to music.

Danny had a car; a Ford Escort. For a teenager, it was a pretty nice car. While hanging out with my friends around town, he would drive by where we were, tell me to get into his car, ride around a few blocks, and then take me back to where my friends were *(if he didn't like the guys who were hanging out with us, he'd ride a lot farther than just a few blocks; he'd drive me to the next town over...around 15 miles from my home)*. The entire time he was driving, he would speed and tell me he didn't want me hanging out with those guys. He would say things like he wasn't going to take me back to my friends and that we were either going straight to my house or his parents' home. I would tell him that if he didn't take me back, I was going to jump out of the car. Most times, my threats would work.

(Would I actually jump out of the car? No! But I said what I knew would work to make him at least take me back home.)

On one particular night, I had been hanging out with my friends. (I would often hide from Danny whenever he would swing by where we were.) I managed to successfully dodge him all night. When it was time to return home, I walked the few blocks back to my house to beat my midnight curfew. As I walked into my yard, he came from out of the darkness from around the back of my house. He jumped on me, knocking me down to the ground. We wrestled and argued about where I had been. He was very upset that he couldn't find me *(this was long before cell phones hit the scene)*. I remember us rolling around in the grass with him on top of me most of the time. He wasn't hitting me; he was holding me down and literally crying because he didn't know where I was or who I was with. His first thought was that I was with another guy.

Luckily, the local drug boy who used to sell to my brother Dwayne drove by, saw Danny on top of me, stopped, and asked if I was okay. Danny quickly got off of me and went home. I went into my house. Usually, after incidents like that, he would buy me gifts or give me money. It wasn't uncommon to get a new Dooney & Bourke bag, my favorite food or candy, brand-name clothes…you name it.

He was so possessive that when I was sick and couldn't go to school, he would skip school and stay home with me. His parents would come to my house in the middle of the night to get him and make him go back home.

Hmm… **NOW** it makes sense to me! I know why his parents didn't like me. I'm sure they thought I had their son acting crazy when, in fact, it was he who insisted on spending his every waking moment with me!

My mom warned me, though. She told me that Danny was possessive and that she wanted me to stop seeing him. Mom said he was no longer welcome at our house, so we started sneaking around to see each other while she was at work. Eventually, all the sneaking became too much for me. Danny found himself another girl to obsess over, and we ended our relationship. This was my first toxic, co-dependent relationship.

I Could Have Killed Him!

I was 18 years old and in my first semester of college when I met Carl. We attended the University of Central Arkansas in Conway. The college was about two hours away from both of our hometowns.

Carl and I met and fell in love quickly. Everything about our lives intertwined early on—how our classes were scheduled, when we would eat throughout the day, our work schedules…**EVERYTHING**. I found myself in yet another co-dependent relationship that became toxic as well. There was hardly a moment when we weren't together and, when we weren't, we knew the exact whereabouts of the other. Eventually, distrust crept its way into our relationship. He would lie about where he was, who he was hanging out with, and when he would be home. We started to argue…a **LOT**. Those arguments turned into wrestling matches.

One night, our wrestling escalated to an outright fight. I grabbed a screwdriver and hit him in the head. He started bleeding. The gash wasn't bad, but it was bad enough to require a trip to the hospital where he received three stitches. I called our parents to let them know what happened. I was terrified! What if I had injured him worse than that? What if I would've killed him? The situation could have ended up really bad.

Well, our relationship didn't get any better after that. We would break up and then get back together…repeatedly. During one of our break-ups, he constantly called me and came over *(I'm sure he thought I had a guy over)*. I wouldn't answer his calls. I wouldn't let him in. One time, he somehow opened and crawled through my apartment window! We argued and fought each other—and that was it. I had decided to fight back in a relationship! The result wasn't any better, but at least I stood up for myself. Not long after this fight, we broke up and never got back together again.

So, What Now?

The pattern of toxicity in my relationships continued throughout my twenties. I even married a man who proved to be just another co-dependent relationship. We started with abusive language towards each other. Sometimes, things got physical. However, early on, we both decided that behavior wasn't healthy and agreed to stop. Unfortunately, that peace agreement didn't last. I endured 20 years of manipulation, financial abuse, isolation, verbal abuse, emotional abuse, and all out being controlled by my husband.

The process of taking my power back began in January 2017 when I told him I wanted a divorce. Presently, I am going through a high-conflict divorce from my narcissistic husband. Through this process, I have found myself again. I'm actually happy—and counting down the days until the divorce is final and my new life can begin.

As cliché as it may sound, I believe ALL things happen for a reason. As I proceed through my healing process, I've learned to trust the process. When things get rough and I want to give up, the following will always be my go-to reminder: **"Trust the process because things do get better!"**

Discussion Questions

1. What do you believe the author's life would have been like had she left those situations earlier?

_____
_____
_____
_____
_____
_____
_____
_____
_____
_____
_____
_____
_____
_____
_____
_____
_____
_____
_____
_____
_____

2. What would be your advice to someone who tells you their relationship "just doesn't feel right"?

CONCLUSION

In closing, I want to emphasize again just how amazing each of the contributors to this project are. They combined the testimonies of their experiences and began not just to transform their own lives; they had the heart and passion for reviving another young girl, young lady, or woman who may be in a similar situation that they have overcome.

****

In life, we aren't afforded the opportunity to pick and choose our life's experiences. In the case of the contributors in *Shade: No More Pain*, we speak on sexual, emotional, physical, spiritual, and verbal abuse—each one a stream of toxicity that could have ended our lives at any time…**BUT GOD!**

As for me, I began to see life differently when I was pregnant at the age of sixteen. I knew some things weren't adding up, which placed me on my journey of wanting to be free. I moved out of my home when I was 16 and began raising my daughter on my own (she was only two months old at the time). I knew I wanted something better for her than what I had experienced:

- ❖ Rejection
- ❖ Abandonment
- ❖ Isolation
- ❖ Lacking in self-love

Initially, when I recognized those things in my life, they scared me—that was until the day I was introduced to Jesus

Christ. That moment just felt "right." Even in the midst of my confusion and fear, a breath of fresh air entered my soul. From that day forward, I vehemently sought God's face and pieced together a yearning for a relationship with a sovereign being I didn't even know...yet. Attending church every Sunday permitted not only fellowship with others; I also felt a piece of me growing in areas I would never have imagined. I started reading God's Word more by getting up each day and making doing so a priority. I longed to know what He was saying to and about **ME**. Soon after, self-love filled my spirit-woman.

As the years progressed, I learned that those things I experienced in life that were intended to break me were going to be used by God to help other young girls, young ladies, and women who looked like **ME**.

In 2014, *Positive Express* was founded. **Positive Express** is an organization that is geared towards helping young girls and young ladies recognize that self-esteem matters. They learn to be transparent with themselves and undo or stop the generational curses that have been imposed upon their identity, causing the wisdom of God to be decreased in their lives. Special emphasis is placed on them knowing that God created each of them in His image.

> *"...and have put on the new self, which is being renewed in knowledge in the image of its Creator."*
> ~ **Colossians 3:10, NIV** ~

Once that has been fully embraced, participants begin to see themselves differently, their actions will display our

Heavenly Father, and the transforming of their minds will be renewed with wisdom to accomplish success in life!

Without a doubt, we will all continue to encounter bumps and bruises along life's highway. Adversity comes to everyone. What makes the difference? It's how we **CHOOSE** to posture in the midst of it all.

> *"Do not be conformed to this world, but be transformed by the renewal of your mind, that by testing you may discern what is the will of God, what is good and acceptable and perfect."*
> **~ Romans 12:2, ESV ~**

On this journey, know that **YOU** no longer have to hide behind the pain.

~ *Tosha R. Dearbone* ~

Decree and declare:

I no longer have to hide behind the pain. I will be a voice to speak up for others.

APPENDIX

Karon, J. (n.d.) Retrieved March 7, 2019, from https://www.brainyquote.com/quotes/jan_karon_489875

Kaur, R. (n.d.) Retrieved March 7, 2019, from https://quotecatalog.com/quote/rupi-kaur-how-you-love-yo-ga4LbNa/

Keller, H. (n.d.) Retrieved March 7, 2019, from https://www.allgreatquotes.com/motivational-1/

Racine, J. (n.d.) Retrieved March 7, 2019, from https://www.brainyquote.com/quotes/jean_racine_398801

Sentamu, J. (n.d.) Retrieved March 7, 2019, from https://www.brainyquote.com/quotes/john_sentamu_545751?src=t_new_life

www.ingramcontent.com/pod-product-compliance
Lightning Source LLC
Chambersburg PA
CBHW052146110526
44591CB00012B/1877